Old Master Drawings
from the
Malcolm Collection

Old Master Drawings

from the Malcolm Collection

Martin Royalton-Kisch
Hugo Chapman
Stephen Coppel

Published for the Trustees of the British Museum
by British Museum Press

© 1996 The Trustees of the British Museum

Published by British Museum Press
A division of The British Museum Company Ltd
46 Bloomsbury Street, London WC1B 3QQ

British Library Cataloguing in Publication Data
A catalogue record for this book is available from the British Library

ISBN 0 7141 2610 1

Designed by Andrew Shoolbred
Typeset in Aldus
By Wyvern Typesetting Ltd
Printed in Belgium
By Snoeck-Dvcaju & Zoon
FRONTISPIECE Michelangelo, *Epifania* (no. 24).

Contents

Preface

Just over a hundred years ago, in 1895, Parliament voted a special grant of £25,000 to the British Museum so that it could acquire the collection of prints and drawings formed by John Malcolm of Poltalloch. Containing almost one thousand drawings and more than four hundred prints, its purchase was the last of a series of remarkable acquisitions made by the Department of Prints and Drawings with the aid of special grants from the Treasury. Its approval was doubtless helped by the fact that the price asked was well beneath the value of the works. No less than eight special grants from the Treasury were made to the Department of Prints and Drawings during the nineteenth century; without them, it would not hold its position among the greatest print rooms of the world.

The Malcolm collection was considered a pre-eminently important addition to the British Museum's holdings of old master drawings primarily because of the masterpieces it contained by Botticelli, Leonardo, Michelangelo, Rembrandt, Claude and Watteau. All these artists are represented in the present catalogue and exhibition, in which an attempt has also been made to reflect the general character of the collection. Minor masters also found their place, provided that, in the words of Malcolm's own guidelines, they were 'exceptionally fine and well-preserved examples'. The collection contained few cursory sketches, and most of the drawings have a finished, pictorial quality.

The earlier Italian schools, from Fra Angelico to Michelangelo, appealed to Malcolm above all, as they had to his early adviser, Sir J.C. Robinson. Indeed Robinson sold his own collection of drawings to Malcolm in 1860, and their tastes were similar. Malcolm's financial resources were greater, based on his lands in Scotland and successful speculations in Australia. When finally acquired by the British Museum, the collection could to some degree be described as the joint product of these two men, although when purchasing drawings Malcolm acted with increasingly independent judgement.

The exhibition contains two hundred of Malcolm's drawings and one hundred are reproduced in this catalogue. The selection has been made by three members of the staff of the Department: Martin Royalton-Kisch has acted as editor and provided the entries for the French, German and Netherlandish drawings; the introductory essay by Stephen Coppel is a reduced version, though with some additions, of the text he prepared for *Landmarks in Print Collecting: Connoisseurs and Donors at the British Museum since 1753*, published in 1996; the entries for the fifty-three Italian and Spanish drawings are by Hugo Chapman.

Two leaves from the Sforza Book of Hours are included in the exhibition, kindly lent by the British Library Board, and our thanks are due in particular to Janet Backhouse for this generous loan. The book, a masterpiece of Renaissance illumination, was the pearl of Malcolm's collection, and its donation to the British Museum by Malcolm in 1893 smoothed the path of the drawings in 1895.

We have enjoyed the assistance of Malcolm's descendants and of colleagues in other institutions; their help is more fully acknowledged by Stephen Coppel in his essay. We would also like to thank our photographer, Graham Javes, and both Coralie Hepburn and Julie Young of British Museum Press.

Antony Griffiths KEEPER

Introduction: John Malcolm of Poltalloch (1805–93)

The present catalogue celebrates the centenary of the acquisition by the British Museum of the outstanding collection of old master drawings formed by John Malcolm of Poltalloch (fig. 1). Purchased at a favourable price in 1895, this acquisition of almost one thousand drawings helped considerably to elevate the Museum's old masters to the same level of quality as the celebrated collections in the Louvre in Paris, the Albertina in Vienna and the other chief repositories of drawings in Europe.

The purchase, which included Malcolm's collection of more than four hundred old master prints, was one of the triumphs of Sidney Colvin's keepership of the Department of Prints and Drawings (1883–1912), which also saw the arrival, again in 1895, of the comprehensive collection of early German woodcuts formed by John Malcolm's close friend William Mitchell, and the bequest in 1910 of the smaller but choice collection of drawings and prints formed by the Australian-born collector George Salting.

William Mitchell and John Malcolm were lifelong friends whose collections complemented each other. They were both connoisseurs of the most discriminating kind and prominent members of the Burlington Fine Arts Club, London's most prestigious venue for collectors in the second half of the nineteenth century. While this essay focuses on John Malcolm, Mitchell's role as a collaborator in the formation of their respective collections cannot be wholly excluded from the story.[1] Mitchell (1820–1908) is said to have made a fortune from sheep-farming in Australia. A somewhat retiring figure, he resided in London for most of his life. He never married and was buried at Poltalloch, the Scottish estate of his close friend John Malcolm.

In Sidney Colvin's published recollections, he described Malcolm as 'a great highland laird, whose passion as a collector [was] to a large extent stimulated as well as directed by an inseparable *fidus Achates* in the person of a bachelor friend of education (and I believe origin) partly German, William Mitchell [. . .]'.[2] Several years Mitchell's senior, John Malcolm was born in 1805, a younger son of the 12th Laird of Poltalloch, Neill Malcolm, who had extensive Highland holdings in Argyll and profitable sugar and rum interests in Jamaica. John Malcolm was educated at Harrow and then at Christ Church, Oxford, where he received his BA in 1827, proceeding to MA in 1830. In 1832 he married Isabella Wingfield Stratford and lived as a country gentleman outside Maidstone, Kent, where he served as a magistrate. During this period he formed an extensive collection of ornithological specimens.[3]

On the death of his elder brother Neill in 1857, Malcolm succeeded to the title of 14th Laird of Poltalloch

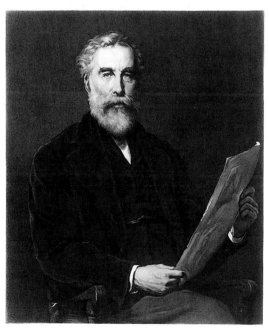

Fig. 1 T.L. Atkinson after W.W. Ouless, *John Malcolm of Poltalloch*, mezzotint, c.1860, 352 x 302mm. 1931-5-8-2, presented by Sir Ian Malcolm.

at the age of fifty-two. He inherited the Poltalloch seat, a stately pile of more than one hundred rooms built by his brother near Lochgilphead, Argyll, in the early 1850s.[4] Malcolm also inherited the family's grand London residence at 7 Great Stanhope Street, off Park Lane. It was here from the 1860s that he entertained his connoisseur friends and enjoyed the pleasure of showing them the treasures of his cabinet. Below the great staircase hung the large and celebrated Michelangelo cartoon (no.24).

A year after his succession in 1857, his wife died; companion marble busts of Malcolm and his wife were commissioned and completed in Rome that year by the sculptor Laurence Macdonald (that of Malcolm is now in the Manchester City Art Gallery). How frequently Malcolm travelled to Italy is unknown, but most of his energies as a collector were devoted to Italian old master drawings.

Unlike his fellow collector Mitchell, whose probated wealth amounted to £20,386, John Malcolm commanded a vast fortune which was valued at £413,046 at his death in 1893. While a measure of his wealth derived from his inherited estates in Scotland and the West Indies, it was the success of his landed ventures in the new colony of South Australia that consolidated his fortune and provided him with the purchasing power necessary to form his collections. In 1839 his brother Neill had purchased a 'Special Survey' of 4,000 acres in the district of Lake Alexandrina, near the mouth of the River Murray. The Special Survey was an opportunity for absentee landlords to invest in the young colony founded in 1836. On payment of £4,000 the purchaser selected an area of 15,000 acres outside the settled districts. Once this had been fully surveyed the investor could take 4,000 acres for himself and offer the remainder to other settlers at the set price of £1 per acre. In the late 1830s, when tenants on the Malcolm estates and elsewhere were enduring severe famines and poverty through forced enclosures in Scotland, relief from their distress through resettlement in South Australia appeared an attractive scheme to Scottish landlords. But when the Highlanders preferred hardship in Argyll to relocation at the other end of the world, the Malcolm brothers decided to convert their newly acquired land into grazing property.[5]

Called 'Poltalloch' after the family seat in Scotland, the cattle station in South Australia became a highly successful enterprise. It was controlled by Neill and then John Malcolm from London through Samuel Davenport, their conscientious agent in the colony, who later became one of its most prominent politicians. John Malcolm acquired further holdings in the area of Lake Albert, near the original holding at Lake Alexandrina: in 1860 he made three separate purchases of land to form a second cattle station called 'Campbell House' of nearly 8,000 acres.

The Australian 'Poltalloch' features in Anthony Trollope's account of his travels in Australia between 1871 and 1872. He described it as 'a large cattle-station in the south of the colony, on the eastern side of the lakes. It belongs to a rich Scotch absentee landowner who sits in our parliament, and I will only say of it that I think I ate the best beef there that ever fell in my way'.[6] In June of the following year, 1873, Malcolm sold his Australian holdings together with 4,000 head of livestock for the enormous sum of £175,000.[7]

It is not inconceivable that it was the business side of Malcolm and Mitchell's landed interests in Australia that brought the two collectors together. Certainly from the 1860s we find their names linked, and the person who was instrumental in helping to direct their taste was the great Victorian connoisseur Sir John Charles Robinson (1824–1913). Appointed in 1852 as superintendent of the art collections at the new South Kensington Museum (later renamed the Victoria and Albert Museum) until the controversial abolition of his post in 1867, Robinson matched his passion for objects with an unrivalled eye for quality.[8] Aside from the purchases made for the Museum in his official capacity, he also played a key role in helping connoisseurs to form their collections.

In 1860 Robinson sold to John Malcolm his outstanding collection of Renaissance drawings, an exceptional event and one that laid a solid foundation for Malcolm's old master drawings cabinet. Although no details of this transaction have survived,[9] the extent of the collection that changed hands can be reconstructed from the catalogue of Malcolm's drawings prepared by Robinson in 1869. Of the 870 works it describes, no less than 554, or two-thirds, are said to have come from Robinson.[10] Although there was a number of Dutch drawings, Robinson's former collection concentrated on works by the Italian Renaissance masters. For example, there were thirteen sheets attributed to Leonardo da Vinci, twenty-three to Michelangelo and thirteen to Raphael. The two last-named artists were the focus of Robinson's seminal catalogue, *A Critical Account of the Drawings by Michel Angelo and Raffaello in the University Galleries, Oxford*, published a year after the Malcolm catalogue in 1870.

Robinson had acquired many of his drawings from the London dealers Messrs Woodburn, who had bought the famous collection of Sir Thomas Lawrence from the latter's executors in 1835 for £16,000. Lawrence's will, written two years before his death in 1830, directed his executors to offer the collection of drawings to the nation for £18,000; but despite the efforts of a public subscription, neither Parliament nor the Treasury would sanction the purchase, while the Trustees of the British Museum and the National Gallery were lukewarm in their support of the public appeal.[11]

In the years immediately following Malcolm's purchase of 1860, Robinson continued to advise him on additions to his collection. At the Woodburn sale of June 1860 he bought on Malcolm's behalf, for as little as £11-0s-6d, the large cartoon by Michelangelo that Woodburn had kept in an oak frame behind plate glass (no. 24).[12] In March 1866, on Robinson's recommendation, Malcolm acquired no less than 135 lots, mostly seventeenth-century Dutch drawings, from the Gerard Leembruggen sale in Amsterdam, one of the most significant private collections to have been formed in the Netherlands in the nineteenth century. Three months later Robinson acted as one of Malcolm's two buyers at the posthumous sale of the Oxford divine Dr Wellesley, at which Malcolm purchased some eighty-three lots, including twenty-four drawings by Claude Lorrain. According to a list Malcolm himself drew up in 1866, his collection by then contained 708 old master drawings arranged in fifteen boxes. In addition there were ten framed works, including the Michelangelo cartoon, three unspecified drawings by Rubens and a Dürer.[13]

Robinson undertook to keep an eye out for Malcolm for further acquisitions during his travels in Spain, adding in one letter written prior to his departure, 'I sincerely hope we shall both be long spared to continue a pursuit which has already during many years been an unfailing

Fig. 2 Folio from the Sforza Book of Hours (Hours of Bona Sforza), *c.*1490: Giovan Pietro Birago, *Martyrdom of St Peter Martyr* (f.205v); on vellum, 131 x 93mm. Courtesy of the British Library Board.

source of pleasurable occupation and instruction to me'.[14] It was in Spain in 1871, in highly dramatic circumstances, that Robinson purchased one of the great treasures of Italian Renaissance illumination, the Sforza Book of Hours (fig. 2). When Malcolm finally gave the manuscript to the British Museum in 1893, as will be discussed below, Robinson related the story of how he had first acquired it:

I forthwith engaged Don José [Robinson's Spanish agent who had already lost 20,000 pesetas by a theft from his pocket upon a previous attempt to buy the book] to get me sight of the ill-omened treasure; this he undertook to do, and the very same evening he brought the priest [the aristocratic owner's chaplain] to my room, when with much ceremony the little corpulent velvet-covered volume was put into my hands. The very first page opened, disclosing two glorious illuminations, blazing with colours and gold, struck me dumb with admiration, but when every page of the book, and there were more than two hundred of them, was revealed equally enriched, the only thought was that it should not again for an instant leave my hands; and literally it did not, for luckily I had provided the funds in anticipation and so the bargain was instantly concluded. No entreaty could induce the vendor to give any information as to the previous ownership or history of the book, although I left no means of persuasion untried[15]

The Sforza Book of Hours was first offered by Robinson to the British Museum, but when the Treasury refused to provide the asking price of £2,500, Malcolm stepped in and bought it for his collection. It was by far the most important item in Malcolm's collection of illuminated manuscripts, which never approached his old master drawings in importance.

The rationale behind the formation of Malcolm's collection of drawings was unequivocally stated in Robinson's preface to the 1869 catalogue (reprinted in an augmented edition in 1876). Robinson distinguished between the choice specimens found in the Malcolm collection and those of eighteenth- and early nineteenth-century collectors, whose 'vast gatherings usually consisted of drawings of doubtful authenticity, or of little intrinsic value, such as academy studies, drawings by unknown and obscure masters, copies by engravers and young artists, etc'.[16] Robinson believed that the encyclopaedic collecting of drawings should properly be left to museums and public institutions, whose 'primary object [is] to illustrate in full detail the entire range of art'. The modern connoisseur, on the other hand, should be more disciplined and selective. In this respect the Malcolm collection in 1869 was a model cabinet. Robinson enumerated the four rules which he and Malcolm had tacitly observed when forming their collections, namely:

1. Irrespective of authorship, to collect only specimens of indisputable excellence as works of art.

2. To aim more particularly at the acquisition of authentic works of the *greatest* masters, and especially of drawings bearing the signatures of their respective authors.

3. In the case of less eminent masters to retain only exceptionally fine and well-preserved examples.

4. To select by preference works, the authenticity and relative importance of which were in a measure guaranteed by the fact of their having passed through celebrated collections of former times, as evidenced by the collectors' marks and written inscriptions upon them.

These criteria equally applied to Malcolm's print-collecting, which he saw as supplementing his primary interest in drawings. It is also of interest to see how much weight was given to provenance as a guarantee of authenticity, a view that has since been increasingly undermined.

Robinson's activities on behalf of Malcolm should be seen in the context of the Burlington Fine Arts Club, the meeting place of like-minded connoisseurs that Robinson had helped to found in 1866.

The origins of the Club go back ten years earlier, when a select group of collectors led by Robinson would gather informally in the evenings, initially at Marlborough House and then at its successor, the South Kensington Museum, but more frequently in private residences. From 1857 this association of gentlemen-collectors became known as the Fine Arts Club. Among its founding members were Robinson as Honorary Secretary, John Ruskin, Felix Slade and Augustus Wollaston Franks of the British Museum.[17] The German scholars G.F. Waagen of Berlin and Professor Ludwig Grüner of Dresden were elected in 1857; the future Liberal Prime Minister W.E. Gladstone, who had developed a taste for blue-and-white porcelain, became a member in 1859. Malcolm was elected in 1862 and Mitchell joined in 1868, but already by the end of 1860 membership of the Club stood at two hundred. Its purpose was to hold *conversazioni*, as these gatherings were called, in members' homes, where the host would make his collection available for inspection and discussion by members and their guests. Members also brought along objects relevant to the previously announced theme of the evening. For more than one of these receptions Malcolm threw open his house at 7 Great Stanhope Street.[18]

The growth of the Fine Arts Club and the increasing social ambition of the *conversazioni* led, on 12 June 1866, to the formation of the Burlington Fine Arts Club at 177 Piccadilly, opposite Burlington House, from which the Club took its name.[19] Robinson was on the inaugural Committee and the Club's founder-members included Malcolm, Mitchell, Franks and Francis Seymour Haden, the etcher and connoisseur of Rembrandt prints. In 1870 a lease was taken out on premises at 17 Savile Row, where the Club remained until 1943. It was here that the connoisseurs of the London art world met and discussed their collections, collaborated or competed for objects and exchanged the latest art world gossip over wine and cigars.[20]

On 9 April 1867 John Malcolm, proposed by Seymour Haden, became a member of the Club's Committee, which considered and decided on proposals for exhibitions and ratified the appointment of newly elected members. As a new Committee member, Malcolm almost immediately found himself embroiled in the heroic feud between Haden and Whistler that ruptured the Burlington Fine Arts Club in its first year. Whistler, elected a member in March, was expelled on 13 December for having assaulted Haden, whom he had pushed through a plate-glass window during a brawl in a Paris café. The expulsion led to the resignation of Whistler's friends the Rossettis, but was ratified by the Committee on 19 December.[21]

Nevertheless, the Club continued to expand its membership. In June 1867 Malcolm and Robinson recommended the election of G.F. Waagen as a permanent honorary member of the Club, a tribute to the German scholar's international standing (his *Treasures of Art in Great Britain* had been published in London in 1852–7).[22] The day after Whistler's expulsion saw the nomination of George Reid, the Keeper of Prints and Drawings in the British Museum, who was duly elected on 27 December 1867. (He resigned seventeen years later after a quarrel with his proposer, Richard Fisher, over the latter's failure to deliver a print catalogue commissioned by the Trustees of the British Museum.)[23]

Malcolm's business acumen made him a powerful and practical member of the Committee in securing the Club's finances. In 1871, to foot the bill of £2,500 for renovating the Club's newly acquired Savile Row premises, debentures were offered to Club members for £125, entitling the holder to an annual interest of four per cent. Robinson, Malcolm, Mitchell and Salting were among the thirty-six members who took out these debentures by 1876.[24] Year after year Malcolm was appointed to the Club's Finance Sub-Committee and throughout the 1870s and 1880s both he and Mitchell regularly served on the General Committee, with Mitchell taking the chair on various occasions after his election to the Committee in May 1875.

The principal business of the Committee was the organisation of exhibitions, and to a degree the collecting interests of Malcolm and Mitchell determined the type of shows that were staged at the Club during the 1870s and early 1880s. The most ambitious of its earliest displays was that of Raphael and Michelangelo drawings arranged by Richard Fisher in 1870.[25] Of the fifty-seven Raphaels exhibited, twenty-three were lent by Malcolm while the second largest number (eighteen) came from the Royal Collection at Windsor. Malcolm also provided seventeen and Windsor fourteen of the forty-eight Michelangelos. Mitchell lent two Raphaels, including the *Ascension of Our Lord from the Tomb*, which he had acquired from under the nose of Fisher at the Hippisley sale two years earlier.[26]

Malcolm lent regularly to the Club's exhibitions in the 1870s. A number of his Claude drawings, acquired at the 1866 Wellesley sale, were shown at an exhibition of the artist's drawings and etchings held at the Club in 1872. The Sforza Book of Hours (fig. 2) was the centrepiece of an exhibition of illuminated manuscripts in 1874 and no less than eighty-seven of Malcolm's purchases from the 1866 Leembruggen sale were lent to the Club's Dutch master drawings exhibition of 1878.[27] One of the most successful exhibitions was Haden's Rembrandt etching show of 1877, which attracted 3,379 visitors, not including members.[28]

It has already been described how Malcolm established the core of his collection of drawings by purchasing Robinson's cabinet *en bloc* in 1860. For its subsequent development, the most important document is a typescript copy of Malcolm's record of the drawings he acquired from July 1865. The

Fig. 3 Follower of Jan van Eyck (*c.*1390–1441), *Supposed portrait of Philip the Good of Burgundy*, silverpoint on prepared, cream-coloured paper, 215 x 144mm. 1895-9-15-998.

chronological listing breaks off on 24 June 1891 with the purchase, for £236-5s-0d, of a Raphael bistre sketch of the *Virgin and Child with an Angel* from the Brooke collection. As Malcolm died two years later, this Raphael acquisition effectively concluded his collecting career.[29] Although the list only specifies the drawings and the prices paid for them, it does give the place and date of each sale and the lot numbers of each item purchased.

In May 1875 Malcolm and Mitchell ventured to Paris to attend the celebrated sale of Emile Galichon (1829–75), the former editor of the *Gazette des Beaux-Arts*, whose important collection of prints and drawings was being sold off following his recent death. Malcolm's purchases concentrated on Galichon's Italian Renaissance prints, apart from a Leonardo da Vinci sketch and two Michelangelo black chalk drawings, one of them being a study for the *Last Judgement*, which he acquired for 5,000 francs each through his agent, Colnaghi's.[30] Not to be outshone, Mitchell acquired the silverpoint portrait of Philip the Good for 6,000 francs, a drawing that was then thought to be by Van Eyck and had been the subject of a scholarly article by Galichon (fig. 3).[31] It was later bought by Malcolm for

14,500 German Marks (or £725) when Mitchell disposed of his old master drawings in 1890. It was the highest price of the sale and by far the highest sum paid by Malcolm for any of his drawings, almost £200 more than its nearest rival in price, a Raphael. This has turned out to be one of Malcolm's few serious errors of judgement as the drawing is now considered to be an indifferent work of van Eyck's school and is no longer thought to represent Philip of Burgundy.[32]

Malcolm and Mitchell also attended the sale of prints belonging to K.E. von Liphart (1808–91) in Leipzig which began on 5 December 1876. In Leipzig Malcolm could, as always, afford to pay more than Mitchell, and he acquired an engraving by the Master BM (Bartsch 1) for 1,501 German Marks, three times the highest price paid by his friend.[33] With his superior purchasing power, Malcolm created a national sensation at the 1884 St John Dent sale in London, when his agent Thibaudeau bid to £860 for the *Assumption of the Virgin* (B.XIII.86.4), a Florentine engraving then attributed to Botticelli, for which Eugène Dutuit of Rouen was the underbidder.[34]

Botticelli was already represented in Malcolm's collection by the celebrated drawing of *Abundance* (no.10), and with the story of Malcolm's acquisitions now outlined, the character of the collection of drawings as a whole can be described. It was of course dictated to a considerable extent by the guiding principles that Robinson and Malcolm had laid down and published in the first, 1869 edition of the Malcolm catalogue. Nonetheless, like all collections it has certain unique characteristics, some of which may be enumerated here.

First, more than four hundred (or forty per cent) of the drawings are Italian, and of these, well over half date from before the death of Michelangelo in 1564. A high proportion, around one-quarter of all the Italian drawings, are fifteenth-century works and it is chiefly from these that the Malcolm collection derives its reputation. The highlights, apart from the Botticelli, include many of the best-known drawings in the British Museum by Fra Angelico, Mantegna, Ghirlandaio, Perugino, Verrocchio and many others. From the High Renaissance, Malcolm could boast some of his most extraordinary groups of works by individual masters. No less than thirty drawings were attributed to Michelangelo in the 1876 Malcolm catalogue (including the cartoon, no.24). Leonardo (16 sheets), Raphael (27), Fra Bartolommeo (17) and Andrea del Sarto (10) were also represented in great strength, and although the attributions in the Malcolm catalogue have not always remained unchallenged, most have stood the test of time.

The later Italian masters were less evenly represented, and Malcolm never acquired Mannerist drawings of comparable importance, apart from those (of a Raphaelesque cast) by Correggio (22). There were only six works given to Francesco Parmigianino, for example, an elegant draughtsman whose drawings were plentiful on the market. The occasional sheet by Domenico Beccafumi, Francesco Salviati, Francesco Vanni, and Giorgio Vasari, and the stronger group of studies by Baccio Bandinelli, do not disguise their comparative unfashionability, and they were not particularly sought out by Malcolm. Of the Italian Baroque, the Carracci and Guercino dominate with eleven and twelve sheets respectively, but in general the field is also markedly less well represented than the High Renaissance. Once again, this runs counter to what was available to nineteenth-century collectors, as does the almost complete omission of eighteenth-century drawings, apart from the three by Canaletto.

After the Italian, the Dutch and Flemish drawings were the most assiduously collected, and over 350 were acquired. The earlier period was here relatively neglected in favour of the seventeenth century, which was fully represented by a broad cross-section of styles, whether Rembrandtesque,

Rubensian, or Dutch Italianate. The tally of drawings by individual artists was headed by Rembrandt with an extraordinary series of thirty sheets, about one-third of which are now attributed to his pupils, followed by Rubens (18), Van Dyck (16) and Nicolaes Berchem (14).

Of the remaining schools, Malcolm appears to have been reluctant to explore beyond those artists who have always been universally esteemed. Thus of the thirty-three German drawings, more than half were attributed to Dürer and Holbein (with eleven and nine sheets respectively). With sixty-five drawings, the French school was only marginally more representative and there were only three works earlier than the seventeenth century. Claude Lorrain, with twenty-six drawings, clearly appealed strongly to Malcolm, but the fine series of fourteen sketches by Antoine Watteau made a greater impact on the collections of the British Museum, where Claude was already well represented through the bequest of Richard Payne Knight in 1824. Finally, there were twenty-four drawings by Spanish artists, including one by Goya. The majority came from Robinson's collection and, with the exception of the Goya, date from the seventeenth century. Murillo was particularly well represented, with six drawings. This was as strong a group as he owned by any of the Italian Baroque masters, apart from the Carracci and Guercino.

Although Malcolm built up an exceptionally rich and important collection, he cannot be described as an innovative connoisseur, and in general his enthusiasms followed the established taste of the time. Yet his collection is so large that it contains enough variety to avoid any sense of dull predictability. As this catalogue demonstrates, the range of draughtsmanship that appealed to Malcolm was broad. His taste embraced works, for example, by Carpaccio, Lelio Orsi, Morazzone and Baglione among the Italians, and Goltzius, Wierix, Lambert Doomer and Slingelandt among the Dutch. It must also be allowed that the collector's strict guidelines could not invariably be matched in the market-place. In choosing the drawings for this publication and the exhibition, we were able to discard from consideration a greater number of indifferent sheets than we had anticipated, whether by important or minor masters. These drawings are of a quality that appears to fall short of his ideal criteria; they are not rough sketches or *primi pensieri*, which as the first of the guidelines might suggest ('[. . .] to collect only specimens of indisputable excellence as works of art') are rarities in Malcolm's collection. Yet to the specialist, the presence of these lesser items only enhances the interest of the drawings, particularly when viewed within the context of the British Museum's collection as a whole. Furthermore, it should be remembered that although Malcolm collected drawings above all, he assembled not only the large group of prints already mentioned but distinguished objects in other fields, including Limoges enamels, a St Porchaire faience *biberon* from the Pourtales collection, various *objets d'art* and an especially fine group of Venetian Renaissance glass.[35]

The Keeper, Sidney Colvin, was assiduous in his efforts to steer the two complementary collections of Malcolm and Mitchell in the direction of the British Museum. In his reminiscences written long after he had retired, Colvin reflected that 'it is a chief part of [the curator's] duty to win the regard and confidence of private collectors, to help and stimulate them in their pursuits, putting his knowledge at their disposal but making them feel the while that their prime, their binding, duty is to acknowledge such help by destining their collections in the long run to enrich the institution which he serves'.[36] An acquaintance of both men from his earliest days at the British Museum, Colvin was well aware of their stature as collectors; he encouraged their fields of collecting and attended the opening of the principal London sales in their company.[37] In 1893, like Reid before him, Colvin joined the Burlington Fine Arts Club where he was assured of an opportunity to befriend the most prominent connoisseurs of the day.[38]

On 30 May 1893, at the age of eighty-eight, Malcolm died at his Poltalloch estate in Argyllshire. Only days before, he had presented the magnificent Sforza Book of Hours to the Manuscripts Department of the British Museum (now part of the British Library). This gift was the subject of a lengthy column in *The Times*, possibly written by Colvin himself or by the Principal Librarian, E.M. Thompson, who was also a friend of Malcolm. The author of the unsigned piece was at pains to point out how Malcolm's munificence repaired the earlier failure by the British Museum to buy the manuscript when it had been first offered to the Trustees by J.C. Robinson in 1871, but warned the Treasury that 'a Malcolm is not always standing by'.[39]

Shortly after Malcolm's death, speculation was rife among connoisseurs and museum officials concerning the fate of his collections of prints and drawings. Malcolm, according to the terms of his will of 2 May 1888, had bequeathed them to his eldest son John Wingfield Malcolm, with the freedom to dispose of them should he so wish. But should his son not be induced by 'special circumstance' to part with the collection, Malcolm expressed the wish that 'they might be kept together and remain in the family as they have for years afforded me much pleasure and are of themselves of very considerable value'.[40]

Once again an article appeared in the columns of *The Times* arguing for the necessity of keeping Malcolm's collection intact for the benefit of the nation:

[S]ince the unfortunate refusal of the Treasury authorities half a century ago to acquire the unequalled collection of sketches and studies by old masters formed by Sir Thomas Lawrence, no second amateur had brought together a cabinet of equal importance with that formed during the last 30 years by Mr. Malcolm, buying at first under the advice of Sir Charles Robinson, and more recently on his own judgment.[41]

Colvin, it appears, had already prepared a plan to avert the danger of a possible dispersal by public sale. In all likelihood it was he or William Mitchell who persuaded Malcolm's heir to deposit the collection on loan in the Department of Prints and Drawings. On 15 June 1893 John Wingfield Malcolm wrote to the Principal Librarian of the British Museum offering the loan on the condition that 'I should wish them used for the benefit of students under such restrictions as the authorities of the Museum and Mr. Mitchell on my behalf may determine'. The same letter continued: 'I would also ask the Trustees to accept from me the cartoon by Michael Angelo which formed part of the collection.'[42] These arrangements were duly announced in *The Times* on 17 July 1893 when the spirit of public duty shown by Malcolm's heir was gratefully acknowledged.[43] By this manoeuvre not only was the collection preserved in one place, it was also made available for amateurs to study in the Print Room like any other part of the permanent collection. Moreover, the spectacular gift of the Michelangelo cartoon gave the Museum a powerful advantage when it later applied to the Treasury for a grant to purchase the Malcolm collection for the nation.

In order to draw public attention to the richness of the Malcolm cabinet, Colvin mounted an extensive display of 450 old master prints and 500 drawings at the British Museum, which opened in March 1894. Almost two-thirds of the exhibition was drawn from Malcolm's collection, and his items were readily distinguishable from the Museum's own holdings by a special Malcolm stamp on

Fig. 4 The 'Malcolm Cabinet'.

the exhibition mounts. Colvin's catalogue, which ran into a second edition by 1895, contained some 568 entries and prominently credited those with a Malcolm provenance.[44]

Anxious to resolve the question of the collection's ultimate destination, in September 1894 Colvin sought the advice of Mitchell, who was then travelling in Italy. From the Grand Hotel in Venice, Mitchell forwarded Colvin's letter to the heir, adding in his reply to the Keeper that 'for the present there is not, I think, any idea of selling, but Harcourt's new succession laws may make it necessary or expedient later on. I saw him last night in the Piazza with Labouchere'.[45] One month later, on 19 October 1894, the Poltalloch heir outlined to Colvin the dilemma he faced on entering his inheritance:

Everyday I find something that must be redone, & now it is much of the Home Farmsteading where walls & roofs are giving way. Thus as things are I cannot afford to do what I should like to do namely make it over to the nation as the Malcolm collection in memory of my dear father. What am I to do? If I sell it, it will be scattered abroad. If I let the Museum pick what it wants, the rest will not sell at a fair price. If it were possible for the Museum to purchase the whole collection at a moderate price & then sell off what it did not want that seems a way out of a difficulty but I believe that is not possible. Sorely against my wish I only see a regular big sale but I should like you & Thompson [the British Museum's Principal Librarian] old friends of my fathers to give me your advice.[46]

The younger Malcolm, prior to his departure early in December to supervise his interests in the West Indies, sought an interview with Colvin in London to hear his suggestions. Shortly after his return to England, John Wingfield Malcolm wrote on 30 May 1895 'after our conversation today' to inform Colvin of his decision 'that the collection of Drawings & Prints made by my late father should become the property of the nation at the price of £25,000 on the condition that each drawing or print should be marked as belonging to his collection'.[47] It is clear that William Mitchell's advice to the heir was also crucial to the success of these negotiations with Colvin. The example of Mitchell's munificence in giving his collection of early German woodcuts to the British Museum in January 1895 doubtless instilled a reciprocal feeling in J.W. Malcolm, and helped smooth the way for his ultimate decision to allow the collection to join Mitchell's in the British Museum at a favourable price.[48]

On 6 June 1895 Colvin recommended to the Trustees the acceptance of the heir's offer, and after the Trustees' special application to the Treasury for a purchase grant, Parliament eventually voted the sum of £25,000 to acquire Malcolm's collection for the nation.[49] Officially made over on 15 September, the prints and drawings were registered with the numbers 1895–9–15–1 to 1448, the first 436 items being the prints; and in accordance with the heir's wishes, they were stamped with Malcolm's name, both on the works themselves and on the mounts (L.1780–81). Malcolm's own mark, which usually appears on the *versos* (L.1489) – the letters IM either side of a tower, based on the Malcolm family device – was probably applied earlier. The drawings came together with the handsome mahogany cabinet – still known as the 'Malcolm cabinet' in the Department – in which the collector must have kept them (fig. 4). Although its provenance is unknown, the cabinet relates closely in design to the desk in the Library at Cranbury Park, Hampshire, designed by J.B. Papworth (1775–1847) in around 1831. The interior of the Malcolm cabinet appears to have been specially adapted with shelving for the drawings.[50]

Looking back on his career, Colvin remarked: 'the purchase of [Malcolm's] treasures for the British Museum after his death almost doubled the importance of the department I had the honour to serve.'[51] The decisions of Mitchell and of Malcolm's heir to place the two collections in the same institution were intended both as a way of keeping them together and of preserving the memory of the collectors' mutual passion for prints and drawings. Today Malcolm's life-size Michelangelo cartoon (see frontispiece and no. 24) and Mitchell's equally large bird's-eye view woodcut of Venice by Jacopo de' Barbari hang on permanent display in the Department of Prints and Drawings at the British Museum. By their impressive scale, superlative quality and art-historical importance, they epitomise the connoisseurship that forever binds the two friends as collectors.

Stephen Coppel

Notes

1 This introduction is a reduced and edited version of my essay on both Mitchell and Malcolm published as chapter 7 in Antony Griffiths (ed.), *Landmarks in Print Collecting: Connoisseurs and Donors at the British Museum since 1753*, British Museum, London, 1996. This also includes my essay on George Salting. I would like to reiterate my debt to Jim Andrighetti (State Library of New South Wales, Sydney), Mrs Necia Gilbert, Adelaide, Professor John Ritchie (Australian Dictionary of Biography, Canberra) and Irena Zdanowicz (National Gallery of Victoria, Melbourne) for their assistance in tracing biographical information concerning these three collectors. Nicholas Turner (J. Paul Getty Museum, Malibu) kindly put me in touch with Malcolm's descendants and informed me of the whereabouts of Mitchell's burial-place. Francis Russell of Christie's also helped with information about the Malcolm family, as did Stephen Cottle of Sotheby's. The assistance of the archivists in the British Museum, Janet Wallace and Christopher Date, was also vital.

2 Sidney Colvin, *Memories and Notes of Persons and Places 1852–1912*, London, 1921, p. 207.

3 A privately distributed family memoir compiled by Dugald Malcolm, 'Neill Malcolm XIII Laird [and] John Malcolm XIV Laird of Poltalloch' (c.1992), has largely provided me with these biographical details. A copy of this document was kindly presented by its author, Malcolm's great-grandson, to the Department's library.

4 A century later Poltalloch was unroofed and abandoned by its heirs after a displenishment sale forced upon them by inheritance laws.

5 See Eric Richards, 'The Highland Scots of South Australia' *Journal of the Historical Society of South Australia*, 4, 1978, esp. pp. 33–9. My account of Malcolm's South Australian venture is derived from 'The Malcolms of the Lakes' in R. Cockburn, *Pastoral Pioneers of South Australia*, II, Adelaide, 1927, pp. 192–3, and the more recent and more accurate archival research conducted in the Land Titles Office, Adelaide by Necia Gilbert and presented in her unpublished 1981 paper, 'John Malcolm of Poltalloch (1805–1893): a great collector with South

Australian connections', a copy of which she has kindly given to the Department. I am also grateful to Julie Robinson, Art Gallery of South Australia, Adelaide for providing references to George C. Morphett, 'The Malcolms', *Royal Geographical Society of Australasia, South Australian Branch*, 43, 1942, pp. 13–15, and J.D. Somerville, 'The Malcolms: a preliminary investigation', typescript, State Library of South Australia (Mortlock Library), Adelaide.

6 Anthony Trollope, *Australia and New Zealand*, II, London, 1873, ch. 12, p. 216. The Duke of Edinburgh (the brother of the future King Edward VII), on his royal visit to the Australian colonies in 1867, was a guest in November at the two Malcolm properties in South Australia. John Malcolm appears not to have been in Australia at the time, although when he renewed Davenport's power of attorney in April 1868 he is recorded as being temporarily resident in Adelaide (Gilbert, *op. cit.*).

7 Malcolm's landed interests in Australia were sold to the Bowman brothers of Crystal Brook, South Australia, whose descendants still own Poltalloch.

8 For an outline of Robinson's career, see his obituary in *The Times*, 11 April 1913, p. 9, and the entry in the *Dictionary of National Biography, 1912–1921*, pp. 471–2. For a recent assessment of his influence as a connoisseur, see the unpublished D.Phil. dissertation by Helen Davies, 'Sir John Charles Robinson (1824–1913): his role as a connoisseur and creator of public and private collections', D.Phil. Oxford, 1992. I am grateful to Dr Davies for allowing me to read her dissertation.

9 J.C. Robinson's Account Book, preserved amongst his papers in the Ashmolean Museum, Oxford, only covers the later period, 1874–1907. See Davies, *op. cit.*, pp. 377–8.

10 J.C. Robinson, *Descriptive Catalogue of the Drawings by the Old Masters, Forming the Collection of John Malcolm of Poltalloch, Esq.*, London, privately printed at the Chiswick Press, 1869. A second edition appeared in 1876 with additional drawings and some amendments of attribution by Malcolm, who also added a new preface.

11 See J.C. Robinson's account of the dispersal of the Lawrence collection and the Woodburn purchase in *A Critical Account of the Drawings by Michel Angelo and Raffaello in the University Galleries, Oxford*, Oxford, 1870, pp. xviii–xxiv.

12 Samuel Woodburn sale, Christie's, 4 June 1860 and following days, lot 160. Robinson's comments on the low prices achieved at the sale are worth recording (*op. cit.*, p. xxiv): '... although a special grant of money was made by the Treasury to the British Museum for the purpose of acquiring the finest works in the sale, so little understanding was there of the paramount value and importance of the specimens on the part of those charged with the disposal of the grant, that a large proportion of incomparable drawings of Michel Angelo and Raffaello, (specimens equal if not superior in importance to those actually acquired), passed into the hands of private collectors at little more than nominal prices, whilst after

the sale a sum of several hundred pounds, sufficient to have purchased them twice over, was actually returned to the Treasury as an unexpended balance.'

13 John Malcolm, 'List of Drawings, 1866' is preserved in the Argyll and Bute District Archives, Kilmory, Lochgilphead; I am grateful to Murdo MacDonald, Senior Archivist, for providing me with a copy of this holograph MS. This document contains two separate listings of Malcolm's cabinet arranged by school in boxes. In both cases the artist and number of sheets are specified but the individual drawings are not described. The first list appears to be of Malcolm's Robinson acquisitions made before 1866, and records 498 drawings kept in ten solander cases under the arrangement of early Flemish and German (box 1), Dutch and Flemish (boxes 2 and 3), early Italian (box 4), Italian (boxes 5 to 9), Spanish, French and English (box 10). The second list includes the Malcolm additions from the 1866 Leembruggen sale. The collection had now expanded to 708 works housed in fifteen cases. Both lists antedate the acquisitions made by Malcolm at the Wellesley sale of June–July 1866, as the twenty-four Claudes are not included.

14 J.C. Robinson, letter to John Malcolm of Poltalloch, 1865, in the Robinson papers, the Ashmolean Museum, Oxford; cited by Davies, *op. cit.*, p. 386.

15 See J.C. Robinson, 'The Sforza Book of Hours', *Bibliographica*, I, 1895, pp. 433–4. For a recent short picture book, see Mark Evans, *The Sforza Hours*, British Library, London, 1992.

16 Robinson, *Catalogue of the Drawings ... of John Malcolm of Poltalloch, op. cit.*, 1869, p. v, where Robinson's other remarks quoted in this paragraph also appear.

17 For a brief history of the Fine Arts Club, see Ann Eatwell, 'The Collector's or Fine Arts Club 1857–1874. The first society for collectors of the decorative arts', *The Decorative Arts Society*, 18, 1994, pp. 25–30.

18 Malcolm's first reception, on 8 June 1865, was attended by sixty-nine members and forty-three guests, including Felix Slade and two British Museum officials, W.H. Carpenter, Keeper of Prints and Drawings, and Augustus Wollaston Franks. The themes for the evening were 'Enamels of Limoges, Damascene Work in General, Art Bronzes, Carved Ivories and Sèvres Porcelain'. The Victoria and Albert Museum, National Art Library, London. Fine Arts Club, General Committee Minute Book, 2, 8 June 1865; Signature Books for the *Conversazioni*, 2, 8 June 1865. He hosted another gathering on 27 April 1870. The elections of Malcolm and Mitchell are recorded in the Candidates' Proposal Book (April 1857–20 June 1872).

19 For a brief history of the Club, see the excellent editorial 'The Burlington Fine Arts Club', *The Burlington Magazine*, 94, 1952, pp. 97–9. When it was finally wound up in 1951, the Club's records were deposited in the V&A National Art Library, London. I have drawn heavily on them for the earlier years in the following account of Mitchell and Malcolm's roles in the Club.

20 Shortly after the Club was founded, Fisher and Haden were entrusted 'to provide the supply of wines, refreshments, cigars etc' (General Committee Minute Book, I, 29 December 1866).

21 Burlington Fine Arts Club Candidates' Books, 1, Whistler proposed 22 February 1867, elected 12 March 1867. See Katharine A. Lochnan, *The Etchings of James McNeill Whistler*, New Haven and London, 1984, pp. 145–6. The events of the Whistler affair are recorded under 1867 in vol. 1 of the Club's General Committee Minute Books.

22 Burlington Fine Arts Club General Committee Minute Book, 1, 25 June 1867.

23 Candidates' Books, 1, Reid proposed 14 December 1867, elected 27 December 1867. Reid's resignation is recorded in the Club's General Committee Minute Book, 2, 12 February 1884. Proof sheets of Fisher's *Catalogue of Nielli and Italian Engravings of the XV Century in the British Museum* and his *Catalogue of Engravings by Marcantonio and Agostino Veneziano*, printed by order of the Trustees in 1883–4, are in the Department's library.

24 'List of Debenture Holders and Interest', 31 December 1876, in Correspondence Relating to the Burlington Fine Arts Club's Debentures and Debenture Holders, 1871–1911.

25 *Raphael Sanzio and Michel-Angelo Buonarroti*, exhibition catalogue, Burlington Fine Arts Club, London, 1870.

26 As recorded by Richard Fisher in a letter to Reid of 25 May 1868 (British Museum, P&D Letter Books, vol. 9). The drawing was no. 32 in the Burlington Fine Arts Club exhibition of 1870. Mitchell disposed of his old master drawings in Frankfurt on 7 May 1890, when the Raphael (lot 93) sold for DM1,190. Acquired by Louis Bonnat, it is now in the Musée Bonnat, Bayonne (repr. Paul Joannides, *The Drawings of Raphael, with a complete catalogue*, Oxford 1983, no. 304).

27 *Exhibition of Drawings and Etchings by Claude Le Lorrain*, exhibition catalogue, Burlington Fine Arts Club, 1872; *Illuminated Manuscripts Catalogue*, exhibition catalogue, loc. cit., 1874; and *Exhibition of Drawings by the Dutch Masters*, exhibition catalogue, with an introductory essay on Dutch drawings by Frederick Wedmore, loc. cit., 1878.

28 *Catalogue of the Etched Work of Rembrandt*, exhibition catalogue, with introductory remarks by Seymour Haden, Burlington Fine Arts Club, 1877. Malcolm was not himself a lender on this occasion. The catalogue was acknowledged as 'one of the most instructive and interesting of those that have been issued by the Club' (General Meeting Minute Books, 1, 28 May 1878, which also records the high visitor numbers). The Rev. C.H. Middleton's contribution to the scholarly catalogue is also recorded, although it is nowhere mentioned in the publication, and this later led to a public rift between him and Haden.

29 John Malcolm, 'Memorandum of the prices paid at different times for Drawings in my collection' (July 1865–24 June 1891); a typescript copy of this twenty-five-page document was given to the Library of the Department of Prints and Drawings by Malcolm's son-in-law, the Hon. A.E. Gathorne-Hardy, in 1911. The running total of the prices paid (with those from foreign sales converted to English sterling) came to £9,422.4s.5d for the period covered. The Raphael is P&G.18 (1895–9–15–637).

30 Emile Galichon sale, Paris (Hôtel Drouot, M. Clément), 10–14 May 1875. The drawings that Malcolm purchased were Leonardo's *Study of a Winged Figure; Allegory with Fortune* (lot 167, F2,025), pen and brown ink and brown wash over sketches drawn with a stylus, 1895–9–15–482, Popham and Pouncey 104; Michelangelo's *Fall of Phaeton* (lot 15, F5,000), 1895–9–15–517, Wilde 55; and Michelangelo's *Studies for the 'Last Judgement'* (lot 16, F5,000), 1895–9–15–518, Wilde 60.

31 Emile Galichon sale, 10 May 1875, lot 49, purchased through Colnaghi's. For the article, see Emile Galichon, 'Des Dessins de Maîtres à propos d'un prétendu portrait de Philippe le Bon, attribué à Simon Marmion', *Gazette des Beaux-Arts*, 22, 1867, pp. 78–90. The drawing is there tentatively attributed to Marmion, although the engraving of it describes it as anonymous. The identification of Philip the Good was also regarded by Galichon as little more than a possibility, but in his sale catalogue it is described without hesitation as by van Eyck and of the Duke of Burgundy.

32 William Mitchell sale, 7 May 1890, Frankfurt-am-Main (Prestel), lot 39. Popham rejected the identification of the sitter as Philip the Good and relegated the drawing to the school of Van Eyck (Popham, 1932, p. 17, no. 1).

33 Other important sales at which Malcolm and Mitchell bought prints were the Firmin-Didot sale, 16 April–12 May 1877, Paris (Hôtel Drouot, M. Pawlowski and MM. Danlos et Delisle) and the Bale sale, Christie's, 9–14 June 1881.

34 St John Dent sale, Sotheby's, 28 March 1884 and the following six days, lot 241. See George Redford, 'Sale of the Dent Collection of Prints', *The Times*, 31 March 1884, p. 8; reprinted in Redford, *Art Sales*, I, London, 1888, p. 368.

35 See the Christie's sale catalogues of 5 July 1894, 1 May 1913 and 8 February 1977. The *biberon* was offered again at the Comtesse de Béhague sale, Sotheby's, Monte Carlo, 5 December 1987, lot 294 repr. (my thanks to Timothy Wilson of the Ashmolean Museum for this information).

36 Colvin, op. cit., p. 205.

37 For example, at the opening of the St John Dent sale which was reported in Redford's 'Sale of the Dent Collection of Prints', *The Times*, 29 March 1884, p. 12 (reprinted in Redford, *Art Sales*, op. cit., p. 368).

38 Burlington Fine Arts Club Candidates' Books, 5, Colvin proposed 11 January 1893, elected 24 January 1893.

39 'The Sforza Book of Hours', *The Times*, 24 May 1893, p. 3.

40 Will of John Malcolm of Poltalloch, 2 May 1888, item 9 (grant of probate 20 July 1893); Somerset House, Probate Registry, London.

41 'The Malcolm Collection', *The Times*, 17 July 1893, p. 5.

42 J.W. Malcolm, letter to E.M. Thompson, 15 June 1893. British Museum, Central Archives, Book of Presents, Supplementary vol. II (January 1890–December 1896). The day prior to the date of this letter, William Mitchell and a friend visited the Print Room, presumably with the purpose of discussing the heir's intentions with Colvin. British Museum, Prints and Drawings Department, Visitors' Book, vol. X (14 June 1893).

43 See n. 41 above.

44 See Sidney Colvin, *Guide to an Exhibition of Drawings and Engravings by the Old Masters, Principally from the Malcolm Collection, in the Print and Drawing Gallery*, exhibition catalogue, British Museum, London, 2nd edition, 1895, p. 4.

45 W. Mitchell, letter to Sidney Colvin, 8 [October] 1894.

46 J.W. Malcolm, letter to Sidney Colvin, 19 October 1894.

47 J.W. Malcolm's letter of offer to Colvin on 30 May 1895 was written on official British Museum notepaper. British Museum, Central Archives, Original Papers, 1895, 2045/2. The collection of prints was always seen as complementing that of the drawings. Malcolm's son-in-law A.E. Gathorne-Hardy had in his possession some prints that were 'Collected to Illustrate the Malcolm Collection of Drawings', according to the catalogue he later produced *(Descriptive Catalogue of Drawings by the Old Masters in the Possession of the Hon. A.E. Gathorne-Hardy, 77 Cadogan Square*, London, 1902, pp. 44–8). Whether these thirty-two prints – mostly early etched facsimiles of drawings or engravings related to works in the collection – actually belonged to Malcolm himself is uncertain.

48 Mitchell's name is recorded with John Wingfield Malcolm in the Department's Visitors' Book, vol. XI, for 30 May 1895, the same day as the heir's letter to Colvin offering the Malcolm collection (see previous note).

49 See 'The British Museum and the Malcolm Collection', *The Times*, 10 July 1895, p. 10. Malcolm had previously given some prints and drawings to his daughter and his son-in-law, A.E. Gathorne-Hardy. The ever-alert Colvin tried to persuade Gathorne-Hardy to part with them, if only by way of an exchange of duplicate prints, but the owner only went so far as to promise to offer them to the Museum first, should he ever decide to dispose of any of them (letter of 28 April 1896 in the Department). Gathorne-Hardy published a catalogue of his collection (see n. 47 above), to which he made some additions. Loans from the collection were made to various exhibitions, and in 1971–2, sixty-nine drawings were exhibited at Colnaghi's in London and at the Ashmolean Museum in Oxford (*Loan Exhibition of Drawings by Old Masters from the Collection of Mr Geoffrey Gathorne-Hardy*, with an introduction by Robert Gathorne-Hardy). The collection then contained about 120 drawings, but has since been sold (Sotheby's, 24 November 1976). What was arguably the most important drawing, Andrea Mantegna's study for his fresco of *St James led to Execution* (destroyed in the Second World War) in the Ovetari Chapel in the Church of the Eremitani in Padua, came to the British Museum in 1976 in lieu of estate duty and with the assistance of the bequest of Richard William Tuck (1976–6–16–1).

50 As pointed out by Martin P. Levy of H. Blairman and Sons Ltd (letter dated 9 November 1993 to Dora Thornton of the Department of Medieval and Later Antiquities), who refers to the article by Edward T. Joy, 'A versatile Victorian designer. J.B. Papworth' *Country Life*, 15 January 1970, pp. 130–31, in which the desk is illustrated (fig. 3).

51 Colvin, *op. cit.*, p. 207.

THE CATALOGUE

The catalogue is arranged in the following order of national schools (the same as that employed by J.C. Robinson in the Malcolm catalogue):

Italian	nos	1–50
Spanish		51–3
French		54–63
German		64–70
Netherlandish		71–100

Within these schools, the drawings are arranged according to the dates of birth of the artists represented, although a few slight variations have been allowed to group works by related artists together.

An alphabetical list of artists is on p. 192. A further 100 drawings are included in the exhibition and listed in the Appendix on p. 189.

Selected literature on each drawing is recorded in the entries. Bibliographical abbreviations are used for literature referred to more than once – the full references are given in the Bibliography on p. 191. Exhibitions and their catalogues are referred to both there and in the entries after the abbreviation 'Exh.', followed by the town in which they were held.

Measurements are given height before width.

All the drawings were marked on the *verso* with Malcolm's own collector's mark (L. 1489), apparently before they entered the collection of the British Museum (the mark was already published by Louis Fagan, *Collectors' Marks*, 1883, no. 309). Curiously, none of the Malcolm drawings that remained in the family's possession (in the Gathorne-Hardy collection – see the Introduction, n. 49) bear this mark with the exception of the School of Mantegna, *Standing male nude seen from behind*, sold Sotheby's, 24 November 1976, lot 4. The other marks, L. 1780–81, were applied by the British Museum.

1 Stefano da Verona 1374(?)–after 1438

A seated man looking up

Pen and brown ink, over black chalk. 232 x 210 mm.
PROVENANCE: T. Lawrence (L. 2445); J.C. Robinson; Malcolm (1895–9–15–788).
LITERATURE: JCR 341; A.M. Hind, *Vasari Society*, First Series, IV, 1908–9, 13 and 14; Popham and Pouncey 254; Exh. Nottingham, University Art Gallery and London, Victoria and Albert Museum, *Drawings in the Renaissance Workshop*, 1983, no. 26 (with further literature).

Robinson seems to have been the first to ascribe this double-sided drawing to a North Italian artist. Hind's suggestion that the artist was Stefano da Verona has been generally accepted. It has been proposed that the drawing may be related to the Evangelists painted by Stefano in about 1420–30 in the Rama chapel in San Francesco, Mantua (destroyed in 1942; repr. E. Moench, 'Stefano da Verona: la mort critique d'un peintre', in *Hommage à Michel Laclotte*, 1994, figs 73–6).

Stefano was the leading figure of the International Gothic school in Verona, and his corpus of drawings is larger than that of any of his contemporaries except Pisanello. His drawings are characterised by expressive, rather scratchy penwork and vigorous hatching.

PROPHAETA. DAVID

2 Attributed to
Guido di Pietro, known as Fra Angelico *c.*1400–55

The prophet David playing a psaltery

Pen and brown ink with purple wash, on vellum. 197 × 179 mm. Inscribed: *PROPHAETA. DAVID*
PROVENANCE: H. Wellesley; Malcolm (1895-9-15-437).
LITERATURE: JCR 1; Exh. London, 1894, no. 13; Popham and Pouncey 2; Degenhart and Schmitt, 1968, I-2, no. 369 (with further literature); Exh. London, 1984, no. 1.

Although no drawings certainly by Fra Angelico are known, the quality of the present study has persuaded many critics to accept the attribution. The miniature-like quality of the drawing would not preclude Angelico, because although he worked principally as a painter there are manuscript illuminations by him (see C. Brandon Strehlke, in Exh. New York, The Metropolitan Museum of Art, *Painting and Illumination in Early Renaissance Florence 1300–1450*, 1994–5, pp. 334–9). The drawing has also been given to his most talented follower, the illuminator and painter Zanobi Strozzi (died 1468). The artist here made use of a piece of waste parchment, as on the *verso* there is a fragment of script from an earlier illuminated manuscript.

Fra Angelico was a Dominican friar who divided his time between his religious duties and painting. He worked principally in Florence, most famously in his order's convent of San Marco. He was called to Rome by Nicholas V, and one of the chapels he frescoed in the Vatican still survives.

3 Filippo Lippi *c.1406–69*

A female saint standing

Metalpoint and black chalk, with grey-brown wash, heightened with white, over stylus, on salmon-pink prepared paper. 308 × 166 mm.
PROVENANCE: J. Richardson, senior (L. 2184); B. West (L. 419); T. Lawrence (L. 2445); J.C. Robinson (L. 1433); Malcolm (1895–9–15–442).
LITERATURE: JCR 6; Exh. London, 1894, no. 16; Popham and Pouncey 150; Degenhart and Schmitt, 1968, I–2, no. 360; Exh. London, 1972, no. 111; Exh. London, 1984, no. 5; J. Ruda, *Fra Filippo Lippi*, 1993, no. D8.

The attribution is due to Robinson. No painting is known that relates to this study for a figure, which is possibly the grieving Virgin at the foot of the cross. The monumental drapery and the understated, but intensely expressive gesture of her outstretched hands, recall the mourning women in Lippi's fresco of the *Celebration of the relics of St Stephen* of the early 1460s from the cycle in the Duomo in Prato (repr. Ruda, pl. 154).

Lippi entered the Carmelite order as a boy. Although nothing is known about his training, the dominant influence in his early work are the frescoes by Masaccio. Lippi, whose first documented work dates from 1437, was consistently patronised by the Medici, and although he painted mainly in Florence he completed two major fresco cycles in Prato (1452/3–65) and Spoleto (1466–9). Vasari's lively biography of Lippi included an account of the latter's seduction of a nun, Lucrezia Buti, who gave birth to his son Filippino; this love affair inspired a poem by Browning and a number of paintings by Romantic artists of the nineteenth century.

24

4 Andrea Mantegna *c.*1431–1506

A saint reading

Pen and brown ink, on paper tinted pink. 172 × 70 mm.
PROVENANCE: T. Lawrence (L. 2445); J.C. Robinson; Malcolm (1895–9–15–780).
LITERATURE: JCR 333; Popham and Pouncey 11; Exh. London, Royal Academy, *Andrea Mantegna*, 1992, no. 24 (with further literature).

One of a group of pen drawings that has been ascribed to either Mantegna or Giovanni Bellini. Recent scholarship has supported Robinson's view that this study is by Mantegna. The drawing probably dates from the first half of the 1460s, soon after the artist had moved to Mantua, as the style accords with that of studies related to the engraving, probably executed by Mantegna, of the *Entombment with four birds* (Bartsch 2).

Mantegna grew up and trained in Padua. His early work in the city, the frescoes in the Ovetari chapel in the church of the Eremitani (destroyed in World War II), attracted the attention of Ludovico Gonzaga who invited him in 1460 to be his court painter in Mantua. He was to remain in the city serving the Gonzaga family for the rest of his life.

5   Attributed to
Giovanni Bellini *c.*1431/2–1516

The Pietà

Pen and brown ink with brown wash. 130 × 94 mm. Inscribed upper right: *Udini*
PROVENANCE: T. Lawrence (L. 2445); J.C. Robinson; Malcolm (1895-9-15-791).
LITERATURE: JCR 344; K.T. Parker, *North Italian Drawings*, 1927, pl. 42; Popham & Pouncey 13.

The drawing, catalogued by Robinson as 'uncertain North Italian', was first attributed to a follower of Bellini by Karl Parker in 1927; Popham and Pouncey were inclined to accept an attribution to the master himself. The moving image of the grieving Madonna cradling her son for the last time before laying him in the tomb recalls, in its restrained depiction of grief, Bellini's painting of the same subject of *c.*1470 in the Brera Gallery in Milan (repr. Robertson, pl. XXXVIII). The style of the drawing is still somewhat reminiscent of that of Mantegna (see no. 4), but the freedom of handling, particularly in the changes to the position of Christ's left hand, would support a dating to the 1470s, when the Paduan painter's influence on Bellini became less marked. The wash may, as has been suggested, be a later addition and the abrupt break at the top is disconcerting; but on the other hand passages such as the drapery folds of the cloth below Christ are sensitively handled. A related drawing of the same subject, without any wash, is in the Musée de Rennes (repr. Exh. Modena, Gallerie Estense and Rennes, Musée de Rennes, *Disegno, les dessins italiens du Musée de Rennes*, 1990, no. 11).

6   Attributed to
Giovanni Bellini *c.1431/2–1516*

The head of a man looking up

Black chalk, the outlines pricked for transfer. 389 × 261 mm.
PROVENANCE: T. Lawrence (according to JCR); J.C. Robinson; Malcolm (1895-9-15-591).
LITERATURE: JCR 154; Exh. London, 1894, no. 90; Popham and Pouncey 16; Robertson, 1981, p. 28; Exh. London, 1994, no. 22.

The drawing was attributed to Melozzo da Forlì when acquired by Malcolm, perhaps based on tradition or on the opinion of its former owner and cataloguer, J.C. Robinson. The attribution depended on the resemblance of the drawing to the foreshortened heads of the apostles in the fresco fragments in the Vatican and the Quirinal Palace of Melozzo's *Assumption* (repr. A. Venturi, *Storia dell'Arte Italiana*, 1913, VII (II), figs 20–23). Popham and Pouncey proposed instead that the drawing might be by Giovanni Bellini, comparing the treatment of the hair and beard, and the general type with those of Bellini's early paintings, such as the Vincent Ferrer altarpiece in the church of SS Giovanni e Paolo, Venice (now generally ascribed to his studio), and the *Coronation*, now in the Museo Civico, Pesaro (repr. Robertson, pls XXV and XLVI). This idea, although plausible, is difficult to verify since there are no certain drawings by the artist, and many of those formerly given to him are now attributed to his brother-in-law, Andrea Mantegna. The pricking of the outline was a means to allow the design to be transferred either directly to the surface to be painted, or to another sheet of paper.

Giovanni Bellini dominated the artistic scene in his native city of Venice for well over half a century. His work had a profound influence on the succeeding generation of Venetian painters, notably Giorgione and Titian.

7 Andrea del Verrocchio *c.*1435–88

Head of a woman with an elaborate coiffure

Black chalk (some oiled) and touches of white chalk. 325 × 273 mm.
PROVENANCE: J.P. Zoomer (L. 1511); Count Andréossy (according to JCR); Malcolm
(1895–9–15–785).
LITERATURE: JCR 338; Exh. London, 1894, no. 18; G. Morelli, *Die Galerien zu München und
Dresden*, 1891, p. 350; Popham and Pouncey 258; G. Passavant, *Verrocchio, sculptures, paintings
and drawings*, 1969, no. D5; Exh. London, 1972, no. 116; D.A. Brown and C. Seymour Jr,
'Further Observations on a Project for a Standard by Verrocchio and Leonardo', *Master
Drawings*, XII, 1974, pp. 127–32; Exh. London, 1984, no. 7.

Catalogued by Robinson as North Italian, from the first half of the sixteenth
century, the drawing was first attributed to Verrocchio by Morelli. The
drawing on the *recto* is based on the much less elaborate study, probably
from life, on the *verso*. Both sides are related to the head of a nymph in a
study in the Uffizi, Florence, which seems to have been started by Verrocchio
and finished by Leonardo (repr. Passavant, pl. 95). The Uffizi sheet may be a
preparatory study for a tournament banner painted by Verrocchio for
Giuliano de' Medici in 1475. Although this hypothesis cannot be proven, the
style of the present drawing does accord with the dating of 1475 as the facial
type of the woman is similar to that of the Virgin in Verrocchio's painting
from the period, the *Virgin and Child*, now in the Gemäldegalerie in Berlin
(repr. Passavant, pl. 69). The drawing may well have belonged to Giorgio
Vasari, the sixteenth-century painter and author of the *Lives of the Artists*,
for in his biography of Verrocchio he describes similar drawings of women's
heads in his collection. Studies such as this had a profound influence on
Leonardo's style.

Verrocchio was born in Florence, where he mainly worked, although his
most impressive sculpture, the equestrian monument of Bartolomeo Colleoni,
is in Venice. He was a skilled painter, sculptor and goldsmith. In his well
organised and versatile workshop, Leonardo, Lorenzo di Credi and Perugino
all received their training.

8 Leonardo da Vinci 1452–1519

Study of a drapery for a kneeling woman

Brush drawing in brown and white distemper on brown linen. 283 × 193 mm.
PROVENANCE: J. Richardson, senior (L. 2184); J. Reynolds (L. 2634); T. Lawrence (L. 2445); King of Holland; G. Leembruggen; Malcolm (1895-9-15-489).
LITERATURE: JCR 51; Exh. London, 1894, no. 35; Popham and Pouncey 95; J.K. Cadogan, 'Linen drapery studies by Verrocchio, Leonardo and Ghirlandaio', *Zeitschrift für Kunstgeschichte*, XLVI, 1983, pp. 43-5; Exh. London, 1986, no. 1; F. Viatte, in Exh. Paris, Musée du Louvre, *Léonard de Vinci, les études de draperie*, 1989, no. 7 (with further literature).

In his biography of Leonardo, Vasari described the young artist making brush drawings on linen of small models draped with cloth dipped in clay so that the folds would remain in place. This seems to have been a fairly standard practice in Florentine studios, later used, for example, by Fra Bartolommeo (see no. 20). The pose of the figure suggests that of a Madonna for an *Annunciation* or a *Nativity*.

This drawing, along with similar ones in the Louvre and the Uffizi, all ascribed to Leonardo, pose particular problems of connoisseurship, as it is likely that more than one student was involved with this type of exercise in Verrocchio's studio. Although the present sheet has sometimes been attributed to Verrocchio himself, the similarity of handling to that of drawings still believed to be by Leonardo argues for the retention of the traditional attribution.

Leonardo trained in the studio of Andrea del Verrocchio in Florence. In 1481-2 he went to the Sforza court in Milan, and remained there until 1499. Following the French invasion he left the city, settling in Florence from 1503 to 1506. He returned to Milan in 1506 and stayed there until 1513. In around 1516 he left for France, where he died in the the manor of Cloux outside Amboise.

9 Leonardo da Vinci 1452–1519

Bust of a warrior in profile

Metalpoint, on cream-coloured preparation. 285 × 208 mm.
PROVENANCE: W.Y. Ottley; T. Lawrence (L. 2445); J.C. Robinson; Malcolm (1895–9–15–474).
LITERATURE: JCR 38; Exh. London, 1894, no. 36; Popham and Pouncey 96; Exh. London, 1972, no. 119; Exh. London, 1984, no. 10; Exh. London, Hayward Gallery, *Leonardo da Vinci*, 1989, no. 2; Exh. Florence, Uffizi, *Il Disegno Fiorentino del Tempo di Lorenzo il Magnifico*, 1992, no. 12.5 (with further literature).

The drawing is probably inspired by a lost relief by Leonardo's master, Verrocchio. Vasari in his biography of Verrocchio mentions two metal – probably bronze – reliefs with profile portraits of Alexander the Great and Darius, sent by Lorenzo the Magnificent to the King of Hungary. A terracotta relief now in the Staatliche Museen, Berlin, probably based on one of these lost works, is similar in both type and costume to the present figure.

The dating of the drawing is uncertain, but the general consensus places it in the period 1475–80, when Leonardo, although still closely linked with Verrocchio, was beginning to emerge as an independent artist. Although the composition may rely on an invention by Verrocchio, the physical type of the figure – whose leonine features are underscored by the snarling lion's head on his breastplate – is characteristic of Leonardo.

10 Sandro Botticelli 1444/5–1510

Abundance or Autumn

Pen and brown ink with brown wash, heightened with white, over black chalk, on paper tinted pink. 317 × 253 mm.
PROVENANCE: G. Vasari (?); S. Rogers; Morris Moore; J.C. Robinson; Malcolm (1895–9–15–447).
LITERATURE: JCR 11; Exh. London, 1894, no. 20; Popham and Pouncey 24; Exh. London, 1972, no, 112; Exh. London, 1984, no. 6; R. Lightbown, *Sandro Botticelli, life and work*, 1989, p. 296.

Often counted among the most beautiful Florentine studies of the fifteenth century, the drawing is generally dated to the late 1470s or early 1480s, a few years after Botticelli's painting of *Primavera* in the Uffizi, Florence. The cornucopia and the grapes could allude to the season of autumn and a somewhat similar female figure appears in a painting of this subject by Botticelli's studio, now at Chantilly. The variety of technique is unusually complex for a drawing of this period.

Botticelli was a Florentine painter, best known for his highly wrought and complex allegorical paintings such as the *Birth of Venus* and the *Primavera*.

11   Domenico Ghirlandaio 1449–94

The naming of St John the Baptist

Pen and brown ink. 185 × 263 mm. Inscribed in lower left corner: *R.Ubin* and near the lower edge right of centre: *P: Perugino*
PROVENANCE: Moritz von Fries (L. 2903); Malcolm (1895–9–15–452).
LITERATURE: JCR 16; Popham and Pouncey 70; J.K. Cadogan, 'Observations on Ghirlandaio's method of composition', *Master Drawings*, XXII, 1984, p. 160.

A preliminary study for the fresco in the Tornabuoni chapel in the choir of the church of S. Maria Novella in Florence. This great scheme of decoration, devoted to scenes from the life of the Virgin and the Baptist, was commissioned from Domenico and his brother Davide by Giovanni Tornabuoni in 1485, and work was completed by the end of 1490.

In the fresco the relative positions and poses of the central group are little altered from those in this drawing; the major difference is to the group of women on the right. The subject is taken from the Gospel of St Luke, I, 63: Zacharias had been struck dumb when he failed to believe the word of an angel who announced that his aged wife, Elisabeth, was to bear a son to be called John. When the new-born child was about to be circumcised, the family were surprised by the choice of name and asked Zacharias to confirm it. According to the Gospel, 'he asked for a writing tablet, and wrote, saying, His name is John. And they marvelled all.'

Domenico, with the help of his brothers, ran one of the most successful workshops in Florence. His two major fresco cycles are in S. Trinità and S. Maria Novella in Florence, and he also worked in the Sistine Chapel.

12   Domenico Ghirlandaio 1449–94

A woman turned to the left

Pen and brown ink. 241 × 117 mm.
PROVENANCE: J. Richardson, senior (L. 2184); T. Lawrence (L. 2445); J.C. Robinson; Malcolm (1895–9–15–451).
LITERATURE: JCR 15; Exh. London, 1894, no. 34; Popham and Pouncey 71.

Like the previous drawing, this is a study for the Tornabuoni chapel. It is a preparatory sketch for the woman in the centre of the fresco of the *Birth of St John the Baptist*. In the painting the details of the drapery and the fall of light on the heavy folds correspond closely to the drawing. The related figure, like many in the cycle, is a portrait of one of the Tornabuoni family or a member of their circle, and the artist probably made a separate portrait study for the head.

    Ghirlandaio's meticulous preparatory method can be followed through the surviving drawings related to the Tornabuoni commission: compositional drawings, such as that for *The Naming of St John the Baptist* (no. 11), were followed by more detailed studies like this one, which, in turn, led to the final stage of full-scale cartoons.

13 Pietro Perugino *c.1450–1523*

Head of a man

Black chalk, over stylus indications. 201 × 188 mm. Inscribed, lower left corner: *And di Assisi*
PROVENANCE: Moritz van Fries (L. 2903); J.C. Robinson; Malcolm (1895–9–15–600).
LITERATURE: JCR 163; Popham and Pouncey 190; P. Scarpellini, *Perugino*, 1984, under no. 92.

Robinson, guided by the old inscription, gave this drawing to Andrea di Luigi, an obscure pupil of Perugino. An attribution to his master is more likely, as the drawing is of high quality. The drawing may be a preliminary study for the head of King David in one of Perugino's frescoes in the Cambio in Perugia (repr. Scarpellini, fig. 173), which were commissioned in 1496, but the drawing is lit from the opposite direction. The technique of making a provisional underdrawing with a stylus was later adopted by Perugino's pupil Raphael (see nos 26 and 27).

Perugino was the leading painter in his native Umbria. He worked in Florence and in the 1480s painted in the Sistine Chapel. In about 1494 Raphael became his pupil.

14 Lorenzo di Credi 1456/9–1537

Head of a boy

Metalpoint, heightened with white, on brown prepared paper. 231 × 199 mm.
PROVENANCE: J. Richardson, senior (L. 2183); T. Lawrence (L. 2445); Malcolm (1895–9–15–460).
LITERATURE: JCR 24; Exh. London, 1894, no. 29; Popham and Pouncey 46.

The attribution to Credi was first proposed by Robinson. Studies such as this one, perhaps modelled by a workshop apprentice, were probably drawn as studio exercises rather than in preparation for paintings. The technique of metalpoint was an exacting one: a pointed stylus, usually made of silver, left a mark on the sheet of paper, which had been prepared with layers of ground bone and white lead. Sometimes, as in the case of the Lippi drawing (no. 3), the ground was vividly tinted. It required great precision of handling, as metalpoint could not be easily corrected and, because the line varied little in thickness, the shadows had to be created through subtle variations in the density of the parallel hatching. Credi's characteristically delicate handling of the metalpoint is enhanced by the sparing addition of white heightening.

Credi was a Florentine painter who studied under Verrocchio alongside Leonardo. He worked closely with his master and after Verrocchio's death in 1488 took over the workshop.

15 Giovanni Battista Cima *c*.1459–1517/8

The Redeemer

Brush and green and brown wash, heightened with white, on blue paper. 397 × 193 mm.
PROVENANCE: J.C. Robinson; Malcolm (1895–9–15–803).
LITERATURE: JCR 356; Exh. London, 1894, no. 68; Popham and Pouncey 41; P. Humfrey, *Cima da Conegliano*, 1983, no. 193.

The drawing, for which no related painting is known, is probably an early work dating from the period 1485–90. The physical type and the sculptural quality of the drapery, the latter ultimately derived from Mantegna, are paralleled in Cima's paintings such as the Olera polyptych of about 1486–8 and the altarpiece, dated 1489, now in the Museo Civico, Vicenza (repr. Humfrey, pls 6 and 23). Robinson originally attributed the drawing to Giovanni Bellini; this is understandable as Cima may well have studied with him and his style, particularly at the beginning of his career, owed much to Bellini's example.

Cima worked mainly in Venice, although he painted a number of works for churches elsewhere in northern Italy. He specialised in painting altarpieces and devotional works.

16 Vittore Carpaccio 1460/5–1525/6

A monk and three musicians in a room

Pen and brown ink with brown wash, on faded blue paper. 189 × 277 mm.
PROVENANCE: P. Lely (L. 2092); R. Houlditch (L. 2214); J. Richardson, senior (L. 2183); W.Y. Ottley; T. Lawrence (L. 2445); Malcolm (1895–9–15–806).
LITERATURE: JCR 359; Exh. London, 1894, no. 70; Popham and Pouncey 38; Exh. London, 1972, no. 115; Exh. Nottingham, University Art Gallery and London, Victoria and Albert Museum, *Drawings in the Italian Renaissance Workshop*, 1983, no. 60 (with further literature).

No painting connected with this drawing is known, although the careful description of the objects on the shelf behind the figures, lit from some unseen window on the left, is characteristic of Carpaccio's minute attention to detail in his paintings. Although the drawing cannot be securely dated, a possible indication is provided by the repetition of the seated musician on the left in Carpaccio's altarpiece, dated 1518, in San Francesco, Pirano. Neither a convincing explanation of the subject, nor the reason why the figure of the monk differs in scale from the musicians, have been provided.

Carpaccio seems to have spent his entire career in his native city of Venice. He specialised in cycles of narrative paintings, four of which survive almost complete.

17 Andrea Solario c.1465–1524

The Lamentation

Black chalk, with pen and brown ink and grey wash. 189 × 185 mm.
PROVENANCE: J.C. Robinson; Malcolm (1895-9-15-771).
LITERATURE: JCR 324; C. Loeser, 'I disegni italiani della Raccolta Malcolm', *Archivio storico dell'Arte*, series 2, III, 5, 1897, p. 356; Exh. Paris; Museé du Louvre, *Andrea Solario en France*, 1985, no. 42; D.A. Brown, *Andrea Solario*, 1987, no. 47 (with further literature).

Robinson tentatively suggested that the drawing might be by the sculptor Agostino Busti, il Bambaia (1483–1548). Loeser, following a suggestion of Enrico Costa, published it as Solario in his 1897 review of the Malcolm collection. The drawing is a preparatory study for the signed painting by Solario now in the Louvre (repr. Brown, pl. 142). Although the composition of the painting is similar to that of the drawing there are a number of changes, most notably the reversal of the positions of St John and one of the Maries at the right. The crosses which feature so prominently in the drawing are placed in the right background of the painting, perhaps to allow space for the tomb behind the figures. The Louvre painting, which was virtually unknown before the museum purchased it in 1978, dates from the artist's period in France from 1507 to 1509. Before its reappearance, the drawing had been associated with Solario's painting of the same subject, now in the National Gallery of Art, Washington, painted shortly before his departure for France (repr. Brown, pl. 90).

Solario came from a dynasty of Lombard architects and sculptors. He was probably trained in his native Milan in the workshop of his elder brother Cristoforo, a sculptor. Solario's style was shaped by his period in Venice in the early 1490s and, following his return to Milan, by the work of Leonardo da Vinci. He was the first Italian painter to bring the new Renaissance style to France, where he worked from 1507–9. Solario painted altarpieces and small-scale devotional works, and was a gifted portraitist.

18 Timoteo Viti 1469/70–1523

Studies of a reclining man and draped figures standing by a parapet

The right-hand group in red chalk, with small touches of white heightening (oxidised), the left-hand figure in pen and brown ink, over black chalk. 267 × 425 mm. Inscribed: *124* (twice)
PROVENANCE: J.C. Robinson; Malcolm (1895–9-15–794).
LITERATURE: JCR 347; G. Morelli, *Die Galerien zu München und Dresden von Ivan Lermolieff*, 1891 ed., p. 260; Exh. London, 1894, no. 71; A.E. Popham, 'On a drawing attributed to Jacopo de'Barbari here restored to Timoteo Viti', *Gazette des Beaux-Arts*, period 6, XLI, 1953, pp. 119ff.; Pouncey and Gere 257.

Described by Robinson as 'uncertain early North Italian [. . .] at the end of the fifteenth century', the drawing was correctly attributed by Popham in 1953. The right-hand group drawn in red chalk, which includes St Bartholomew holding a knife, are preliminary studies related to the figures to the right of the Madonna's throne in a drawing of the *Virgin and Child with with saints* in the Kunsthalle, Hamburg (repr. Popham, 1953, fig. 2). Viti had particular trouble resolving the pose of the saint to the left of St Bartholomew: there is a conspicuous correction in his first attempt, and then he tried again with a fainter red chalk study to the left. At some later stage Viti filled the left-hand section of the paper with a carefully finished pen and ink study of a garlanded figure, possibly intended for some mythological composition. This figure is based on a black chalk study, drawn from a model in the same pose but seen from a different angle, now in the Louvre (repr. O. Fischel, *Die Zeichnungen der Umbrer*, 1917, fig. 327).

Viti was born in Urbino and went to Bologna to train first as a goldsmith, and then later as a painter. Although little known as a painter, Viti was a capable draughtsman, and in the past his drawings have been confused with those of Luca Signorelli and the young Raphael. Malcolm owned five drawings by Viti, a suprisingly large number for such a minor artist, although two of them were given by Robinson to Francia and Raphael.

19 Francesco Granacci 1469/70–1543

*The Virgin and Child with Saints Francis, Anthony Abbot
and two others*

Pen and brown ink with brown wash, heightened with white, with traces of squaring in the
central section, on grey prepared paper. 320 × 262 mm.
PROVENANCE: J. Richardson, senior (L. 2184); E. Knight; H. Wellesley; J. Malcolm (1895–9–15–
468).
LITERATURE: JCR 32; C. von Holst, *Francesco Granacci*, 1974. no. 33; Exh. London, 1986, no. 59
(with further literature).

The drawing was catalogued by Robinson as 'Early Florentine School', with a
suggestion that it might be by Mariotto Albertinelli. Frederick Antal
reattributed it convincingly to the Florentine painter Granacci, a pupil of
Lorenzo di Credi and Domenico Ghirlandaio. The altarpiece for which this is
a study is lost; however, three small panels now in the Museo Stibbert in
Florence (repr. von Holst, figs 61–3) might have once been part of its
predella, as the composition of the central one is close to that of the drawing.
In the drawing, the artist has carefully described the form of the altarpiece,
possibly for the approval of the patron, including details of the suggested
cornice and pilaster. From its resemblance to the composition of Granacci's
altarpiece completed in 1522 in the church of S. Giovanni Battista at
Montemurlo (repr. von Holst, fig. 56), the drawing may be dated to the same
period.

Granacci trained in the workshop of Domenico Ghirlandaio alongside
Michelangelo, with whom he was to remain in contact. In 1508 he was called
to Rome by Michelangelo to assist him in the Sistine chapel ceiling, but he
returned to Florence in the same year. His painting style was largely
dependent on that of the previous century, although he was later influenced
by Fra Bartolommeo and Andrea del Sarto.

20 Baccio della Porta, called Fra Bartolommeo 1472–1517

Drapery study for Christ in the 'Last Judgement'

Brush drawing in grey-brown and white distemper on linen tinted grey. 307 × 213 mm. Inscribed lower right: *LEONARDO da Vinci*
PROVENANCE: P. Sandby (L. 2112); W.Y. Ottley; T. Lawrence (L. 2445); S. Woodburn; J.C. Robinson (L. 1433); Malcolm (1895–9–15–487).
LITERATURE: W.Y. Ottley, *The Italian School of Design,* 1832, p. 22; JCR 49; Exh. London, 1986, no. 28 (with further literature); C. Fischer, in Exh. Rotterdam, Boymans van Beuningen Museum, *Fra Bartolommeo, Master Draughtsman of the High Renaissance,* 1990, under no. 6.

Robinson attributed this drawing to Leonardo, although he was aware that its former owners, William Young Ottley and Thomas Lawrence, had given it to Fra Bartolommeo. Ottley had correctly identified it as a study for the figure of Christ in Fra Bartolommeo's fresco of the *Last Judgement,* commissioned by Gerozzo Dini in 1499 for the wall over his mother's grave in the cloister of the hospital of S. Maria Nuova in Florence. The fresco, the most important commission of Fra Bartolommeo's early career, was still uncompleted when he abandoned the profession of painting to become a monk in July 1500. His associate, Mariotto Albertinelli, finished the work on the basis of his drawings. This drapery study was probably drawn, like the Leonardo drawing (no. 8), after a small wooden model draped with cloth dipped in plaster.

Fra Bartolommeo was a Florentine painter who studied under Cosimo Rosselli (1439–1507). He gave up painting on entering a Dominican monastery, but took it up again four years later. After the departure of Leonardo in 1506, he was the leading painter in the city.

21 Michelangelo Buonarroti, called Michelangelo 1475–1564

A philosopher

Pen and brown and grey ink. 331 × 215 mm.
PROVENANCE: J.D. Lempereur; B. Constantine; T. Dimsdale; T. Lawrence (L. 2445);
S. Woodburn; J.C. Robinson; Malcolm (1895–9–15–498).
LITERATURE: JCR 61; Wilde 1; de Tolnay, I, 1975, no. 6; Exh. London, 1975, no. 1; Exh.
Leningrad and Moscow, 1979, no. 28; Exh. New York, 1979, no. 1; Exh. Adelaide and Melbourne,
1980, no. 28; Exh. London, 1984, no. 15; Exh. London, 1986, no. 8 (with further literature).

The use of two shades of ink is an unusual feature and has led some to
question whether the drawing has been retouched. But the homogeneity of
the handling leaves little doubt that the drawing is entirely by Michelangelo.
It probably dates from about 1496 some years later than Michelangelo's
similar, but less fluent, pen copies after figures in frescoes by Giotto and
Masaccio. The brilliant contrast between the densely shaded areas of cross
hatching and the highlights, where the artist has left the paper blank, is
somewhat reminiscent of the shining surface of polished marble. The
identification of the figure is not certain, although the most plausible
suggestion is that he is a philosopher, probably holding a skull. The hat is
derived from that worn by the Byzantine Emperor John Palaeologus, who
visited Italy in 1438–9.

Sculptor, painter and architect, Michelangelo was one of the most gifted
artists of all time. He entered the workshop of Domenico and Davide
Ghirlandaio in 1488. Except for brief periods in Bologna he worked
exclusively in his native Florence and for the Papal court in Rome.

22 Michelangelo Buonarroti, called Michelangelo 1475–1564

Studies of a crucified man (Haman)

Red chalk. 406 × 207 mm.
PROVENANCE: Casa Buonarroti; J.B.J. Wicar; T. Lawrence; S. Woodburn; Malcolm (1895–9–15–497).
LITERATURE: JCR 60; Exh. London, 1894, no. 129; Wilde 13; de Tolnay, I, 1975, no. 163; Exh. London, 1975, no. 23 (with further literature); Exh. Washington and Paris, *Michelangelo Draftsman*, 1988–9, no. 7.

A preparatory study for the figure of the crucified Haman, painted in the spandrel at the altar end of the Sistine Chapel. This belongs to the latest part of the ceiling and was probably executed in 1512. The subject is taken from the Book of Esther, VII, 10: Haman was an enemy of the Jews, but his persecution of them finally led King Ahasuerus to order him to be hanged. The dramatic, highly foreshortened pose studied in this sheet, doubtless drawn from a model, was further refined in a red chalk drawing of the figure's head, neck and shoulders, arms and hands, now in the Teylers Museum, Haarlem (de Tolnay, no. 164). The small chalk circles added by Michelangelo on some of the forms in the present drawing, most visibly on the separate study of the leg at the lower right, seem, as Michael Hirst observed, to be a notation to show the artist the projected areas of strongest highlights in the fresco (M. Hirst, *Michelangelo and his Drawings*, 1988, pp. 67–8).

This sheet, like many of Malcolm's best Italian drawings, once belonged to the painter Sir Thomas Lawrence (1769–1830). Part of Lawrence's collection of drawings, one of the greatest ever assembled, was offered at auction in 1860, following the death of the dealer Samuel Woodburn. Robinson bought a number of drawings in this sale, and these later entered Malcolm's collection. Of the twenty-three authentic Michelangelo drawings from his collection, all but five were once owned by Lawrence.

23 Michelangelo Buonarroti, called Michelangelo 1475–1564

Ideal head of a woman

Black chalk. 287 × 235 mm.
PROVENANCE: Casa Buonarroti; J.B.J. Wicar: W.Y. Ottley; T. Lawrence; H. Wellesley;
J. Addington; Malcolm (1895–9–15–493).
LITERATURE: JCR 56; Wilde 42; de Tolnay, II, 1976, no. 316; Exh. London, 1975, no. 114; Exh.
New York, 1979, no. 15; Exh. London, 1986, no. 83 (with further literature).

This highly finished drawing, dated by Wilde to the second half of the 1520s,
is an example of a presentation drawing, a work of art in its own right
intended as a present. Michelangelo was not the first artist to have made
drawings specifically for this purpose; Leonardo da Vinci, for example, is
recorded as having drawn a *Neptune* as a gift for his friend Antonio Segni in
the early years of the sixteenth century. Yet no other artist of the period
devoted so much time and effort as Michelangelo to producing drawings as
gifts, not to patrons, but to those in his most intimate circle. The
extraordinary refinement of the modelling in this sheet, achieved through a
combination of hatching and stippling, is typical of the artist's painstaking
approach to this type of drawing.

Michelangelo's *teste divine*, as they were described by Vasari, were developed
from an established Florentine tradition. Although stylistically very different,
details such as the elaborately braided hair and the figure's fantastic cap recall
highly finished drawings by earlier Florentine masters, such as those by
Verrocchio and Botticelli in this catalogue (nos 7 and 10). Malcolm also
owned two other presentation drawings by Michelangelo: the *Fall of
Phaethon* (Wilde 55) drawn for Tomasso de'Cavalieri, and the *Christ on the
Cross* (Wilde 67) given by the artist to the Marchesa di Pescara.

24 Michelangelo Buonarroti, called Michelangelo 1475–1564

Epifania

Black chalk, on twenty-six joined sheets. 2327 × 1656 mm.
PROVENANCE: Canon Fulvio Orsini; Cardinal Odoardo Farnese; Cardinal Silvio Valenti; Lucien Buonaparte; T. Lawrence; S. Woodburn; Malcolm, presented by John Wingfield Malcolm, 1893 (1895–9–15–518*).
LITERATURE: JCR 81; Exh. London, 1894, no. 141; Wilde 75; de Tolnay, III, 1978, no. 389; Exh. London, 1975, no. 153 (with further literature).

A cartoon, or full-size preparatory drawing, made by Michelangelo in the early 1550s for a panel painting, now in the Casa Buonarroti in Florence, by his *protégé* and biographer Ascanio Condivi (*c.*1525–74). The unfinished painting is of feeble quality, and this may, apart from the artist's modest talent, be partly due to the fact that the cartoon is neither squared nor indented, so that the design could not have been directly transferred onto the panel. Condivi's difficulties would have been compounded by the lack of finish and the rapid revisions of the outlines that blur the contours. These make the cartoon a difficult model to follow. Condivi was the latest, and least gifted, of those artists who, through their friendship with Michelangelo, received drawings by him to help them prepare their compositions.

The cartoon was among the possessions listed in an inventory following the artist's death, and shortly afterwards the subject was described as an *Epifania*. This would normally refer to the *Adoration of the Magi*, which the cartoon clearly does not represent. In the centre is the Virgin with the infant Christ sleeping between her legs; the Infant Baptist, recognisable through his lambskin, and St Joseph are on the right. The Virgin appears to push St Joseph away as she turns towards the unidentified figure on her right. Together with the other figures behind, recent scholarship has suggested that the cartoon's imagery refers to the brothers and sisters of Christ mentioned in the Gospels. The title *Epifania* could allude to the fourth-century St Epiphanias, who held that they were the children not of the Virgin but of St Joseph by a previous marriage, and that her marriage was never consummated. This would explain her gesture in the cartoon (see E.H. Gombrich, *New Light on Old Masters*, 1986, pp. 171–8).

For the cartoon's acquisition by Malcolm, see the Introduction, p. 9.

Detail, see frontispiece.

25 Baldassare Peruzzi 1481–1536

A group of sibyls

Pen and two shades of brown ink. 309 × 264 mm.
PROVENANCE: Padre Resta (?); T. Lawrence (L. 2445); J.C. Robinson; Malcolm (1895–9–15–763).
LITERATURE: JCR 316; Pouncey and Gere 238; C.L. Frommel, *Baldassare Peruzzi als Maler und Zeichner*, 1967/8, no. 4.

A preparatory study for the right-hand group of sibyls in one of the ceiling compartments of the apse of the church of S. Onofrio, Rome. The fresco decorations, painted between 1502/3 and 1506, are the earliest surviving works by the Sienese painter and architect Baldassare Peruzzi, executed soon after he left his native Siena and established himself in Rome. The two main figures on the right of the fresco correspond closely to those in the drawing, the main differences being the change to the position of the sibyl in the upper-right corner and the omission of the angel. Robinson was unaware of the drawing's connection with the fresco, but his attribution to Sodoma (1477–1549), who worked in Siena and later, like Peruzzi, in Rome for Agostino Chigi, attests to the high quality of his connoisseurship.

Peruzzi's artistic training is not known, but on the evidence of the S. Onofrio frescoes, he was influenced by Pinturicchio's work in Siena. He travelled to Rome *c.*1502, where his most significant early work is the design and decoration of the palatial villa, now known as the Farnesina, commissioned by the Sienese banker Agostino Chigi. Peruzzi was a gifted architect, with a profound knowledge of the antique; much of Sebastiano Serlio's *Libri dell'Architettura* was based on his ideas. His painted works, which have a strongly Raphaelesque flavour, include frescoes in the church of S. Maria della Pace and the Villa Madama.

26 Raffaello Santi, called Raphael 1483–1520

Head of a middle-aged man

Black chalk, over stylus underdrawing. 255 × 190 mm.
PROVENANCE: R. Houlditch (L. 2214); T. Lawrence (L. 2445); King of Holland; Malcolm (1895–9–15–619).
LITERATURE: JCR 181; Exh. London, 1894, no. 100; Pouncey and Gere 8; Exh. London, 1974, no. 35; Joannides, 1983, no. 66; Exh. London, 1983, no. 32 (with further literature).

The purpose of the drawing is unknown, but it can be dated on stylistic grounds to around 1504, based on the figure's similarity to some of the heads in the Brera *Marriage of the Virgin*, completed in that year. The naturalism and high degree of finish of the drawing, evident in details such as the puffy flesh under the eyes, may have been inspired by near-contemporary Flemish paintings, which were collected at the court of Urbino. Raphael's use of stylus underdrawing is particularly evident in this study.

Raphael received his first training from his father Giovanni Santi, a minor painter in Urbino. Soon after 1494 he entered the studio of Pietro Perugino (c.1450–1523), the leading painter of the Umbrian school. From 1504–8 Raphael was in Florence, where he studied the works of Leonardo and Michelangelo and painted a number of panels of the *Virgin and Child*. In 1508 he went to Rome at the invitation of Pope Julius II. He continued to work for the Papal court as a painter, designer of tapestries and architect until his premature death at the age of thirty-seven.

27 Raffaello Santi, called Raphael 1483–1520

Head of a young man gazing upwards

Black chalk over traces of dotted underdrawing. 274 × 216 mm. Inscribed lower right corner: *78* and *94*

PROVENANCE: W.Y. Ottley; T. Lawrence (L. 2445); King of Holland (?); G. Leembruggen; Malcolm (1895–9–15–610).

LITERATURE: JCR 172; Exh. London, 1894, no. 98; Pouncey and Gere 5; Exh. Leningrad and Moscow, 1977, no. 49; Exh. Adelaide and Melbourne, 1980, no. 50; Joannides, 1983, no. 50; Exh. London, 1983, no. 25 (with further literature).

This study corresponds with the head of the apostle, traditionally identified as St James, in the *Coronation of the Virgin*, now in the Vatican. The painting, commissioned by Alessandra degli Oddi for her chapel in the church of S. Francesco in Perugia, is not dated, but the style suggests that it was painted in the period 1502–3, towards the end of the artist's first period, when he was based in his native Umbria.

The drawing represents the final stage of the preparatory process. The standard Renaissance practice was to progress from working drawings to a full-scale cartoon, a drawing of the same size as the intended painting, the outlines of which would be transferred directly onto the final surface either by incising, or by pricking with a pin and sprinkling black chalk powder through the holes. In the present study, based on the evidence of the dots of black chalk visible beneath the chalk lines and the correspondence in size with the finished work, it appears that Raphael pounced the outlines of the head from the cartoon. His intention was to study further those areas of particular importance in the composition. He continued to make slight modifications even after such painstaking preparations, as the head of the figure in the painting is tilted further back and turned slightly further away.

All the surviving examples of this category of drawing – known as auxiliary cartoons – are of heads, two with the addition of hands. Malcolm also owned a rather rubbed auxiliary cartoon for one of the disciple's heads in Raphael's last painting, the *Transfiguration*, now in the Vatican, which confirms Raphael's continued use of this method (Pouncey and Gere 38).

28 Raffaello Santi, called Raphael 1483–1520

Female saint, half-length

Black chalk, over stylus underdrawing. 411 × 260 mm. Inscribed along lower edge: *Raffaelle d'Urbino*

PROVENANCE: W.Y. Ottley; T. Lawrence (L. 2445); King of Holland; H. Wellesley; Malcolm (1895–9–15–612).

LITERATURE: JCR 174; Exh. London, 1894, no. 95; Pouncey and Gere 9; Exh. London, 1972, no. 132; Joannides, 1983, no. 67; Exh. London, 1983, no. 33 (with further literature); Exh. Tokyo and Nagoya, 1996, no. 4.

Robinson's dating of the drawing to *c.*1504, at the end of Raphael's period in his native Umbria, has been followed by all subsequent scholars. The elaboration of the drapery and the facial type are close to those in Raphael's paintings of the period, such as the *Marriage of the Virgin* in the Brera, Milan. The purpose of the drawing is not known, but it may be a study for a lost or unexecuted painting in the manner of his master Perugino's single half-length figures of saints. Again following the example of Perugino (see no. 13), Raphael began the drawing by making a rapid preliminary sketch with a stylus which, because it left only a faint trace on the surface of the paper, allowed him to experiment freely before taking up the chalk.

69

29   Tiziano Vecellio, called Titian   1488/90–1576

Musicians in a landscape

Pen and two shades of brown ink, over traces of black chalk. 224 × 226 mm.
PROVENANCE: J. Six; V. Röver; H. Wellesley; Malcolm (1895–9–15–817).
LITERATURE: JCR 370; Wethey, 1987, no. 35; Exh. Paris, Grand Palais, *Le Siècle de Titien*, 1993,
no. 94 (with further literature).

As with many pen and ink drawings ascribed to Titian, the attribution of this
study has been the source of intense debate. The correspondence between the
woman seen from behind and a figure in the painted *Fête Champêtre*, now in
the Louvre, variously described as a work of Giorgione or Titian, has further
complicated the issue. In the eighteenth century the drawing was given to
Giorgione, but Robinson's attribution to Titian has found general favour,
although some scholars, noting the greyish brown shade of ink used for the
woman, have ingeniously suggested that this part is a preparatory study by
Giorgione for the Louvre painting, and that the rest was completed by Titian
using a darker brown ink. Close examination of the drawing undermines this
hypothesis, as the greyish ink in some areas is clearly on top of the brown
ink. Why Titian used two tones of ink in the right-hand figure is unclear, but
there is no reason to suppose that the drawing was executed in two distinct
stages. On grounds of style, the drawing can be dated to the beginning of the
second decade of the sixteenth century.

    Titian was the most important Venetian painter of the sixteenth century
and his work influenced not only younger painters, such as Tintoretto and
Veronese, but also masters of succeeding generations, like Rubens and
Velasquez.

30 Tiziano Vecellio, called Titian 1488/90–1576

St Peter looking up, his hands joined in prayer

Black and white chalk, on faded blue paper. 157 × 134 mm.
PROVENANCE: J. Reynolds (L. 2364); W.Y. Ottley; T. Lawrence (according to JCR); W. Esdaile
(L. 2617); Malcolm (1895–9–15–823).
LITERATURE: JCR 376; Wethey, 1987, no. 18 (with further literature); Exh. London, Royal
Academy, *The Genius of Venice 1500–1600*, 1983, no. D70; Exh. Venice, Palazzo Ducale, *Tiziano*,
1990; no. 12.

A preparatory study for the seated figure of St Peter in the *Assumption of
the Virgin*, painted for the high altar of the church of S. Maria Gloriosa dei
Frari in Venice. The painting, which was commissioned *c.*1516 and put in
place in 1518, was radically different from the static composition and
contemplative mood of the traditional Venetian altarpiece, perfected by
Giovanni Bellini and his followers. The dynamic upward movement, and the
expressive force of the amazed apostles in Titian's painting, reflect his
awareness of the new artistic developments in Rome, notably the works of
Raphael and Michelangelo.

   The pose of the saint in the painting is essentially the same as in the
drawing, although the drapery is simplified. By exploiting the atmospheric
qualities of the black chalk, the artist has successfully modelled the figure
through varying the density of shade. A few touches of white chalk
highlights, now sadly rubbed, emphasize the sleeve and upturned face.

31 Lorenzo Lotto 1480(?)–1556/7

The Holy Family with angels

Pen and brown ink with brown wash. 177 × 146 mm.
PROVENANCE: Mercer; Whitehead; Malcolm (1895–9–15–684).
LITERATURE: JCR 243; Popham and Pouncey 130; R. Pallucchini, 'Cataloghi', *Arte Veneta*, V, 1951, pp. 194–7; P.M.R. Pouncey, *Lotto disegnatore*, 1965, p. 16; Exh. London, 1994, no. 58.

Ascribed to the Ferrarese artist Dosso Dossi (*c*.1490–1542) when in the Malcolm collection, the drawing was attributed to Liberale da Verona (*c*.1445–1526/9) soon after entering the British Museum. In 1951 it was recognised by Pallucchini as the work of Lotto. The drawing is typical of the artist in the combination of Renaissance forms, notably the pyramidical composition with Christ at the apex, with an intensely felt and highly personal treatment of a sacred theme. Although there is no known related painting, the tremulous gestures of the adoring angels recall those in Lotto's picture of the *Recognition of the Christ Child* of the late 1530s, formerly in the Palazzo Comunale in Osimo (repr. B. Berenson, *Lorenzo Lotto*, 1956, pl. 299), and the drawing may date from about the same period.

Lotto was trained in Venice, where he was greatly influenced by Giovanni Bellini. After a brief stay in Rome he settled in Bergamo in 1512, where he remained until the second half of the 1520s. He was active for the rest of his life in the Veneto, often in the smaller towns in the region, painting portraits and religious works.

32 Attributed to
Benvenuto Tisi, called Garofalo c.1481–1559

Head of a young man

Black chalk. 281 × 263 mm.
PROVENANCE: Earl of Arundel; P. Lely (L. 2092); H. Wellesley; Malcolm (1895–9–15–770).
LITERATURE: JCR 323; Exh. London, 1894, no. 41; P. Pouncey, 'Drawings by Garofalo', *The Burlington Magazine*, XCVII, 1955, pp. 196–200; Exh. London, 1974, no. 24; Exh. London, 1994, no. 41 (with further literature).

When this drawing was in the celebrated collection of the Earl of Arundel, it was given to Leonardo and etched in reverse by Wenceslaus Hollar (1607–77). Hollar omitted the halo and the letters, perhaps because they were rightly judged to be later additions. The drawing has the appearance of a portrait drawing which someone has later tried to transform into an image of St John the Evangelist by the somewhat clumsy addition of a halo. Robinson's attribution of the drawing in the Malcolm catalogue to the Milanese School of Leonardo is understandable, as the *sfumato* lighting and the intent but detached gaze of the sitter are reminiscent of portraits by Leonardo and his circle. In 1955 Philip Pouncey advanced the attribution to Garofalo, a Cremonese artist active in Ferrara, pointing to the similarity of types between this drawing and those in his early paintings, such as the ceiling in the Palazzo di Lodovico il Moro in Ferrara.

33 Giulio Pippi, called Giulio Romano *c.1499–1546*

A battle scene

Pen and brown ink with brown wash, heightened with white, on blue paper, traces of squaring in black chalk in lower-right corner. 253 × 381 mm.
PROVENANCE: Malcolm (1895-9-15-643).
LITERATURE: JCR 202; F. Hartt, *Giulio Romano*, 1958, no. 233; Pouncey and Gere 88; Exh. Mantua, Palazzo del Te and Palazzo Ducale, *Giulio Romano*, 1989, p. 408 (with further literature).

A *modello* for the left-hand group on one long side of the ceiling of the Sala di Troia in the Appartamento di Troia in the Palazzo Ducale in Mantua (repr. Hartt, fig. 385). Painted in 1538, it was the largest of the rooms that Giulio had to decorate in the palace. The size of the task of designing the decorations of the Palazzo Ducale meant that Giulio, as with many of his recently completed frescoes in the Palazzo del Te, had to delegate the work of painting them to his assistants, who made cartoons based on detailed drawings such as the present one. In comparison with Giulio's preparatory drawings, the paintings are of disappointing quality. Under great pressure to complete the decorations, Giulio had little time to check the progress of the work and, as the artist explained in a letter to his patron Federico Gonzaga, one of his assistants, Luca da Faenza, failed to follow his designs.

One of the few sixteenth-century painters to be born in Rome, Giulio entered the studio of Raphael and quickly became one of his most trusted assistants. He was the leading figure in the completion of projects left unfinished at his master's death in 1520, notably the Sala di Costantino in the Vatican. From 1524 until his death in 1546 he was the court artist of the Gonzaga family in Mantua. An innovative architect and a gifted draughtsman, his greatest work is the Palazzo del Te in Mantua which he both designed and decorated.

34 Antonio Allegri, called Correggio 1489/94–1534

Study for Eve in the dome of Parma Cathedral

Red chalk. 183 × 130 mm.
PROVENANCE: P. Lely (L. 2092); Earl of Cholmondeley (L. 1149); J. Reynolds (L. 2364); R. Ford
(L. 2209); J.H. Hawkins (according to JCR); Malcolm (1895–9–15–738).
LITERATURE: JCR 298; Exh. London, 1894, no. 164; Popham, 1967, no. 12; Gould, 1976,
fig. 118c; di Giampaolo and Muzzi, 1988, no. 64 (with further literature).

Correggio was commissioned to decorate the dome of Parma Cathedral with a
fresco of the *Assumption of the Virgin* in 1522, although he did not begin
the work until some years later; the first recorded payment dates from 1526,
the last from 1530. His ability as a painter of illusionistic frescoes was already
proven by his work in the dome of the nearby church of S. Giovanni
Evangelista, but the cupola of the cathedral was far larger and higher, posing
much greater problems in designing a composition that would be clearly
legible. In this early drawing for the figure of Eve, her pose differs greatly
from that of the painting, where she holds the apple in her extended left
hand. The artist probably rejected the idea of an accompanying *putto* holding
the apple, because he recognised that it would have been difficult to identify
Eve without her attribute as she is placed at the top of the dome.

   The artist was born in Correggio some twenty miles from Parma, the city
where he established his reputation.

35   Antonio Allegri, called Correggio   1489/94–1534

Allegory of Vice

Red chalk. 274 × 194 mm.
PROVENANCE: J. Richardson, senior (L. 2184); J. Bouverie (L. 325); J.C. Robinson; Malcolm (1895–9–15–736).
LITERATURE: JCR 296; Popham, 1967, no. 17; Gould, 1976, fig. 181c; Exh. London, Victoria and Albert Museum, *Splendours of the Gonzaga*, 1981–2, no. 115; di Giampaolo and Muzzi, 1988, no. 98 (with further literature).

A highly finished study for the *Allegory of Vice*, painted *c*.1530, which was commissioned by Isabella d'Este for her *studiolo* (little study) in the Palazzo Ducale in Mantua, along with the pendant *Allegory of Virtue* (both now in the Louvre; repr. Gould, pls 180 and 181). Both paintings were executed in tempera to fit in with the works of Mantegna, Perugino and Costa that already hung in the room. The correspondence between the painting and the drawing is close, the only significant difference being the addition of a child's head in the foreground of the picture. The purpose of the study may have been that of a *modello*, to show to the patron for her approval.

    In keeping with Isabella d'Este's sophisticated literary taste, the precise meaning of Correggio's paintings in the *studiolo* is deliberately obscure.

36 Girolamo Francesco Maria Mazzola, called il Parmigianino 1503–40

Figures in a ferry boat

Pen and brown ink with brown wash. 279 × 203 mm.
PROVENANCE: P. Lely (L. 2092); B. West (L. 419); H. Wellesley; J.C. Robinson; Malcolm (1895–9–15–753).
LITERATURE: JCR 310; Popham, 1967, no. 121; A.E. Popham, *Catalogue of the Drawings of Parmigianino*, 1971, I, no. 224; Exh. Leningrad and Moscow, 1979, no. 38; Exh. Adelaide and Melbourne, 1980, no. 38.

Parmigianino was one of the most gifted and prolific draughtsmen of the sixteenth century. Drawings such as this one – most likely a sketch of a remembered scene, rather than one made on the spot – appear to have been made for their own sake. In this respect Parmigianino was unusual, as the majority of sixteenth-century artists drew in order to prepare compositions for finished works and not for their own pleasure.

A native of Parma, the artist received his earliest training from his uncles. Active as a painter, etcher and a designer of engravings and woodcuts, his early work, executed in Parma, was much influenced by Correggio. He later worked in both Rome and Bologna before returning to his native city in the early 1530s. His refined and highly mannered style was enormously influential both in Italy and north of the Alps.

37   Nicolò dell'Abate 1509/12–71

Jupiter and Semele

Pen and brown ink with grey-green wash, heightened with white, over black chalk, and with traces of black chalk squaring, on grey prepared paper. 387 × 289 mm. Inscribed, possibly by the artist: *Semele Giove*
PROVENANCE: R. Houlditch (L. 2214); R. Willet; W.Y. Ottley; T. Lawrence (L. 2445); Malcolm (1895–9–15–678).
LITERATURE: JCR 237.

The attribution to Nicolò dell'Abate can be traced back as far as the sale of Lawrence's drawings in 1860. The drawing is not related to any known work, but it can, on stylistic grounds, be dated to the artist's period in Bologna from 1548 to 1552, when his work was most strongly influenced by Parmigianino (on whom see no. 36). In Bologna, Nicolò would have been able to study drawings and prints by Parmigianino, as well as a number of his paintings, including the *St Roch* in the church of S. Petronio and the *Conversion of St Paul*, now in the Kunsthistoriches Museum, Vienna.

    Nicolò was born in Modena. In 1548 he arrived in Bologna, where his work in the city, such as the decoration of the Palazzo Poggi, led to an invitation to France. From 1552 he collaborated with Francesco Primaticcio (1504–70) for almost twenty years on the decoration of the palace at Fontainebleau.

38 Giorgio Vasari 1511–74

*The Virgin and Child with the infant Baptist, St Jerome, Tobias
and the Archangel Raphael*

Pen and brown ink with brown wash, heightened with white (partly oxidised), on blue-grey
paper. 350 × 226 mm.
PROVENANCE: T. Lawrence (L. 2445); S. Woodburn; J.C. Robinson; Malcolm (1895–9–15–569).
LITERATURE: JCR 132; Exh. London, 1894, no. 159; Exh. London, 1986, no. 140 (with further
literature).

There is no known painting related to this study, but the highly worked
quality of the drawing, with only minor corrections, would suggest that it
was drawn at the last stage in the planning of an altarpiece.

Vasari was born in Arezzo. He worked extensively both in Florence and
Rome, often for the Medici family, and through a large and efficient studio
he managed to produce an enormous body of work. Vasari's activity as a
painter and architect has been overshadowed by his fame as the author of the
Lives of the Artists, first published in 1550 and heavily revised in 1568. It has
remained the essential source for any history of Italian Renaissance art.

39 Follower of Luca Signorelli *c.*1441–1523

An allegorical scene. A page from Giorgio Vasari's *Libro de'Disegni*, attributed by Vasari to Vittorio Carpaccio (1460/5–1525/6)

Pen and brown ink, the border in pen and brown ink with brown wash, over black chalk. 571 × 442 mm (the whole sheet). Inscribed below the drawing: *Anno 1495* and lower right *du Cabinet de Giorgio Vasari & monté par lui même.*
PROVENANCE: G. Vasari (L. 2858); P. Crozat (?); T. Lawrence (L. 2445); J.C. Robinson (L. 1433); Malcolm (1895–9–15–807).
LITERATURE: JCR 360; Popham and Pouncey 249; Exh. London, 1986, no. 143 (with further literature); Exh. Tokyo and Nagoya, 1996, no. 23.

Vasari was one of the first collectors of drawings, and whole pages from his *Libro de'Disegni*, or 'Book of Drawings', have always been highly prized. Vasari appears to have collated his drawings in eight volumes and these complemented his celebrated biographies, the *Lives of the Artists*. The historical approach he adopted in the *Lives* was followed in his collection, with drawings tracing the development of Italian art from Cimabue and Giotto to the artists of his own period. Although biased in favour of drawings from his native Tuscany, his collection included examples by artists from all regions of Italy.

Vasari wrongly attributed the drawing to Carpaccio, as is shown by the inclusion of a proof woodcut portrait of the artist for the revised second edition of the *Lives*, published in 1568. The drawing is now given to a follower of the Umbrian painter Luca Signorelli. Although Vasari sometimes himself drew the elaborate borders surrounding his drawings, the pedestrian quality of the ornamentation in this example would suggest that he left it to a studio hand. Malcolm also owned another page from the *Libro* with drawings attributed by Vasari to the unknown Bolognese artist Galante, which is now ascribed to the Sienese school, second half of the fourteenth century (JCR 239, Popham and Pouncey 269).

VITTORE SCARPACCIA PITT.
VINIZIANO.

Anno 1495

Du Cabinet de Giorgio Vasari & monté par lui même.

40 Taddeo Zuccaro 1529–66

The Flight into Egypt

Pen and grey and black ink with brown wash, heightened with white, over black chalk, on paper washed brown. 394 × 233 mm.
PROVENANCE: W.Y. Ottley (?); T. Lawrence (L. 2445); S. Woodburn; J.C. Robinson; Malcolm (1895-9-15-655).
LITERATURE: JCR 214; J.A. Gere, *Taddeo Zuccaro: his Development studied in his Drawings*, 1969, no. 101; Gere and Pouncey 329.

A study for one of the frescoes flanking the high altar in the church of S. Maria dell'Orto in Rome, painted by Taddeo's brother, Federico, in the late 1550s. The upper section, with the muscular angels straining to pull down the fruit-laden branches within the reach of the Christ Child – a characteristically inventive treatment of a traditional motif – had already been resolved in a study for the same composition in the Louvre. The focus of the present drawing was principally the lower section, as is clear from the many pen and ink revisions to the poses of the figures and the donkey. The informal and naturalistic treatment of the subject may explain the traditional attribution, accepted by Robinson, to Federico Barocci (*c*.1535–1612). The latter, as a young man, did work in Rome with Taddeo, and both artists were from the Marches.

Taddeo was one of the most brilliant Mannerist painters and draughtsmen active in Rome, where he settled at the age of fourteen. He was essentially self-taught and worked extensively in the city on both religious and secular commissions. The Farnese family employed him to paint decorations glorifying their family, both in their Roman palace and their villa at Caprarola.

41 Giovanni Baglione *c.1575–1643/4*

Saint Peter baptising Saint Prisca

Pen and brown ink with brown wash, heightened with white, over red chalk, on blue paper.
377 × 266 mm.
PROVENANCE: P. Crozat; Marquis de Lagoy (L. 1710); Malcolm (1895–9–15–666).
LITERATURE: JCR 225; Gere and Pouncey 36.

From an inscription on another study of the same composition (Zeri collection, Italy), it is clear that the present drawing is related to an unsuccessful attempt by Baglione to win the commission for the main altarpiece of the church of S. Prisca on the Aventine in Rome. The church was redecorated in 1600, and the commission for the painting from Cardinal Benedetto Giustiniani must date from this period. This elaborately finished drawing may have been the form in which the artist submitted his design. In the event, the altarpiece of the same subject was painted by the Tuscan painter Domenico Passignano (1559–1638). In his painting the figures are on the same relative scale as in the present work, and the compositions are broadly similar. A smaller sketch by Baglione for the same composition was acquired by the Department in 1978 (Gere and Pouncey 37).

Baglione is now perhaps better known for his biographies of artists working in Rome, published in 1642, than for his numerous altarpieces, which are executed in a dry, late-Mannerist style.

42 Pier Francesco Mazzucchelli, called il Morazzone 1573–1626

Jacob wrestling with the Angel

Pen and brown ink with brown wash, heightened with white, over black chalk, on blue-grey paper, squared in black chalk. 277 × 246 mm. Inscribed lower right: *tintoretti* and upper left: *N.° 302.*

PROVENANCE: Malcolm (1895–9–15–853).

LITERATURE: JCR 404.

A study for the painting of *c*.1610, now in the Galleria dell'Arcivescovado in Milan (see Exh. cat., Varese, Villa Comunale del Mirabello, *Il Morazzone*, 1962, pl. 72). The subject is from Genesis, XXXII, 23–32: Jacob wrestled with a man from late in the night until dawn. His opponent touched the hollow of his thigh and it came out of joint. Jacob did not yield, and the fight stopped only when dawn broke and the stranger blessed him. Jacob then realised that he had been fighting with an angel.

Morazzone was one of the most original painters working in Lombardy in the early seventeenth century. He studied with the Mannerist painter the Cavaliere d'Arpino (1568–1640) in Rome, before returning to his native Lombardy in the late 1590s.

43   Ludovico Carracci 1555–1619

Virgin and child with angels

Pen and brown ink with brown wash, over red chalk and black lead, the outlines indented for transfer. 167 × 116 mm.
PROVENANCE: Malcolm (1895–9–15–686).
LITERATURE: JCR 245; D. DeGrazia Bohlin, *Prints and related drawings by the Carracci family*, exh. cat., Washington, 1979, under no. 3.

As was first noted by Robinson, this is a study, in reverse, for a print by Ludovico (Bartsch 2; DeGrazia Bohlin 3). The artist experimented freely with the red chalk, most notably in the position of the Christ child's left arm, and then finalised the composition using the pen. The design corresponds closely in size to the print, and Ludovico probably placed the drawing directly on the copper plate and then traced the outlines through to the ground with a stylus. Ludovico made only four prints, and that related to the present drawing probably dates from the late 1590s or early 1600s.

    Ludovico, the uncle of Agostino and Annibale, was the founder of the Carracci Academy, and after the departure of his nephews to Rome he was its uncontested head. Ludovico's Mannerist training became gradually more evident once his nephews had left Bologna, and his refined, linear drawing style strongly marked the younger generation of Bolognese artists.

44 Agostino Carracci 1557–1602

Studies of a landscape with figures by a river, a pair of clasped hands and the head of a boy

Pen and brown ink. 173 × 211 mm. Inscribed lower right, possibly by Cardinal Santa Croce:
AGOSTIN CARRACCI (see J. Labbé and L. Bicart-Sée, *La collection Saint-Morys au Cabinet des Dessins du Musée du Louvre (II)*, Paris, 1987, fig. 12), and numbered above in a different hand: *117*
PROVENANCE: Cardinal Santa Croce (?); P.J. Mariette (L. 1852); Holloway; Malcolm (1895–9–15–696).
LITERATURE: JCR 255; Turner, 1980, no. 36.

The drawing is typical of the classical landscape type established by Annibale and Agostino Carracci, which combined naturalistic elements within a highly orchestrated composition. After finishing the landscape, Agostino used the sheet to make the drawing of a boy, probably from life, with a subsidiary study of his hands to the left. Both Agostino and his younger brother Annibale executed numerous drawings of this type, and the observation of nature and drawings from life were fundamental to the artistic reforms promoted by the Academy that they established with their uncle, Ludovico, in Bologna in the early 1580s.

Agostino collaborated with Annibale and Ludovico on a number of projects in Bologna and later in Rome, as well as painting independent commissions such as the *Last communion of Saint Jerome* in the Vatican.

45 Annibale Carracci 1560–1609

An angel playing a violin

Red chalk. 165 × 202 mm.
PROVENANCE: W.Y. Ottley; T. Lawrence (L. 2445); Malcolm (1895–9–15–723).
LITERATURE: JCR 283; Exh. London, 1894, no. 168; D. Posner, *Annibale Carracci, a study of the reform of Italian Painting about 1590*, 1971, II, under no. 21; Turner, 1980, no. 35.

A study for the angel in the upper right of the altarpiece of the *Baptism of Christ*, dated 1585, in the church of S. Gregorio, Bologna (repr. Posner, pl. 21a). The glowing, *sfumato* tonality of the painting, and the brilliantly foreshortened figures in the upper register reflect Annibale's close study of Correggio's work in Parma. The style of this study, particularly in the delicacy of the modelling, shows that he was strongly influenced by Correggio's drawings (see no. 35). The traditional attribution to Correggio, which was accepted by Robinson, is therefore not surprising.

Annibale, the younger brother of Agostino (on whom see no. 44), was the most brilliant member of the Carracci family. His early work painted in Bologna shows his rapid assimilation of the High Renaissance style that he had studied in paintings in Parma and Venice. He left for Rome in 1595, where he was principally occupied with the illusionistic fresco decorations on the vault of the gallery of the Palazzo Farnese, completed in 1600.

46 Francesco Albani 1578–1660

The death of Adonis

Pen and brown ink with brown wash. 189 × 265 mm.
PROVENANCE: Earl Spencer (L. 1531); J.C. Robinson; Malcolm (1895–9–15–697).
LITERATURE: JCR 256; Exh. London, 1894, no. 204; Turner, 1980, no. 41.

The drawing is possibly a study for a now lost painting of this subject, which is mentioned in the artist's correspondence. The style, particularly in the treatment of the landscape, resembles that of Albani's master, Annibale Carracci. The subject is taken from Ovid's *Metamorphoses*: Adonis, a beautiful youth beloved by Venus, was killed by a boar, which is shown in the drawing escaping to the right.

Albani was a Bolognese painter who received his initial training in the studio of Denys Calvaert (1540–1619), but he later left to study at the Carracci Academy. He worked under Annibale Carracci in Rome, and after the latter's illness took charge of the Herrera chapel commission in the church of S. Giacomo degli Spagnoli, Rome. Although best known as a painter of secular works, particularly small-scale mythological pieces, Albani painted a number of altarpieces for Bolognese churches.

47 Giovanni Francesco Barbieri, called Guercino 1591–1666

Cleopatra

Red chalk. 292 × 215 mm.
PROVENANCE: Casa Gennari; J. Bouverie (L. 325); C. Hervey; 1st Earl of Gainsborough; J.C. Robinson; Malcolm (1895–9–15–709).
LITERATURE: JCR 269; Exh. London, 1894, no. 200; Exh. BM, *Drawings by Guercino from British Collections*, 1991, no. 120 and Appendix 36; Exh. Tokyo and Nagoya, 1996, no. 72.

The drawing can be dated on stylistic grounds to the late 1630s. It cannot be connected with any surviving work, but it may have been a study for one of the two paintings of this subject from this decade which are known through contemporary descriptions, but are now lost (see *La Cleopatra, pittura dell'immortal pennello del Sig. Cav. G.F. Barbieri di Cento*, Forlì, 1638).

Guercino was one of the few Italian Baroque draughtsmen that Malcolm collected, and he owned twelve drawings by the artist (two of which are no longer accepted as autograph). From his collection of seventeenth–century Italian drawings it is clear that Malcolm favoured the more classical style of the Bolognese school: the second largest group after Guercino is that of studies by the Carracci family.

Guercino was the leading painter in Bologna after the death of Guido Reni in 1642. He was a draughtsman of great originality, and his drawings were highly prized by collectors, particularly in England in the eighteenth century. A large number of them, including the present one, can be traced back to the heirs of Guercino, the Gennari, who sold the artist's stock of drawings that they had inherited.

48 Pietro Testa 1612–50

Sinorix carried from the temple of Artemis

Pen and brown ink with brown wash, over black chalk. 285 × 193 mm.
Inscribed: *Piero Testa ft. 1640* and *Pietro Test f.*; numbered in the Crozat hand: *32*
PROVENANCE: P. Crozat; Malcolm (1895–9–15–667).
LITERATURE: JCR 226; Exh. Philadelphia, Philadelphia Museum of Art and Cambridge, Arthur
M. Sackler Museum, *Pietro Testa 1612–1650, prints and drawings*, 1988–9, no. 54 (with further
literature).

This is an early study for the etching (Bartsch 19) before Testa decided on a
horizontal format. The story of Sinorix is recounted in Plutarch's *Mulierum
virtutes*: Sinorix, a powerful tetrarch in Galatia, fell in love with the virtuous
Camma, wife of the tetrarch Sinatus and high priestess of the cult of
Artemis, the goddess of the hunt and of chastity. He murdered Sinatus and
then courted his widow, who finally accepted his suit on condition that her
official pledge took place before the statue of the goddess. Aware of Sinorix's
crime, she offered him a cup of poison after drinking from it herself. Feeling
the effects of the poison, Sinorix hoped that the movement of his chariot
might cure him, but he died that night, and Camma hearing the news expired
rejoicing. In the present drawing the composition is divided equally between
the two protagonists, but in the print Testa concentrated on Sinorix and his
entourage. The inscription on the drawing is not in Testa's hand, although
the date of 1640 may well be correct. The obscure choice of subject is in
keeping with the current taste among the antiquarian circles that Testa
frequented in Rome.

49 Carlo Dolci 1616–87

Self-portrait

Black and red chalk. 279 × 203 mm.
PROVENANCE: Earl Spencer (L. 1530); H. Wellesley; Malcolm (1895–9–15–577).
LITERATURE: JCR 140; Exh. London, 1894, no. 208; Exh. London, 1974, no. 136; Turner, 1980, no. 52.

The traditional identification of the drawing as a self-portrait of the
Florentine painter Carlo Dolci would appear to be confirmed by the similarity
of the sitter's features and those in his painted *Self-portrait* in the Uffizi (F.
Baldassari, *Carlo Dolci*, 1995, no. 141). The highly wrought technique of the
drawing is in keeping with the miniature-like finish in Dolci's paintings.

Dolci was a Florentine artist, whose extreme religiosity is reflected in his
intensely felt, and highly worked religious paintings. His shy and retiring
nature, and the chronic bouts of depression that hastened his death, are
vividly described in Filippo Baldinucci's contemporary biography of the
artist *(Notizie dei Professori del Disegno da Cimabue in qua*, 1847 ed., V,
pp. 335–64).

50 Giovanni Antonio Canale, called Canaletto 1697–1768

A capriccio with the Rialto Bridge

Pen and brown ink, over black chalk. 119 × 237 mm.
PROVENANCE: H. Wellesley; Malcolm (1895–9–15–864).
LITERATURE: JCR 415; W.G. Constable and J.G. Links, *Canaletto*, 1976, no. 766.

The structure with arcades leading up to an arch in the centre is based on the Rialto Bridge, but instead of spanning the Grand Canal the artist has substituted stairs. In the background is a fanciful version of the *campanile* of the church of SS Apostoli. The drawing can on stylistic grounds be dated to the 1730s. The combination of right-handed shading in the lower part of the drawing with left-handed hatching in the sky is unusual. As the latter does not look like a later addition, the artist, who was right-handed, may have turned the sheet.

The most celebrated view-painter of eighteenth-century Venice, Canaletto was trained by his father, Bernardo, a theatrical scene-painter. After a brief period in Rome, Canaletto established himself in Venice, and his first recorded commissions date from the mid 1720s. He was a particular favourite of English collectors, most notably Consul Joseph Smith, and from 1746 to 1755/6 he lived and worked mainly in London. He was a prolific draughtsman, and for a brief period in the 1740s he made a number of etched views.

51 Attributed to
Francisco de Zurbarán 1598–1664

Head of a monk with his eyes closed

Black chalk, with dark grey wash. 277 × 196 mm.
PROVENANCE: José Madrazo, Madrid; J.C. Robinson; Malcolm (1895-9-15-873).
LITERATURE: JCR 424; M.S. Soria, *The Paintings of Zurbarán*, 1953, no. 34; Exh. London, 1974,
no. 79; Exh. London, 1984, no. 149; D. Angulo and A.E. Pérez Sánchez, *A Corpus of Spanish
Drawings, Seville 1600–1650*, 1985, no. 245 (with further literature).

The validity of the traditional attribution to the Sevillian painter Zurbarán is
difficult to assess as there are no certain drawings by the artist. Soria
suggested that it was a study of a dead monk from nature, and that the artist
might have used it for the head of the dead saint in the painting of *Saint
Bonaventura on his bier*, now in the Louvre (repr. Soria pl. 11). There is
some resemblance between the two heads, but the viewpoint is different as
the figure in the painting is seen from the side.

   The artist was born in Seville where he spent most of his life, only
moving to Madrid in his final years. Zurbarán painted religious subjects
almost exclusively.

52 Sebastián de Herrera Barnuevo 1619–71

Assumption of the Virgin

Pen and brown ink with brown wash, squared in black chalk; the paper made up in upper-left corner, and upper-right edge. 250 × 198 mm.
PROVENANCE: José Madrazo, Madrid; J.C. Robinson; Malcolm (1895–9–15–876).
LITERATURE: JCR 427; H.E. Wethey, 'Alonso Cano's drawings', *The Art Bulletin*, XXXIV, 1952, p. 233.

The drawing was attributed by Robinson to Alonso Cano (1601–67), but Wethey's suggestion that it is by his pupil, Herrera Barnuevo, has generally been accepted. No related painting is known, although the sharply raked perspective of the drawing would suggest that it was intended to be seen from below.

Herrera Barnuevo was the son and pupil of the sculptor Antonio Herrera. In the early 1640s he studied under Alonso Cano, and first came to public attention in 1649 when he took part in the preparation of the decorations for the triumphal entry into Madrid of the new Queen, Mariana of Austria. He worked as a painter, sculptor and as an architect. In 1662 he was appointed chief architect to the King, and five years later he succeeded Mazo as the official court painter of King Carlos II.

53 Francisco Goya y Lucientes 1746–1828

King Carlos and Queen Maria Luisa on horseback

Brush and brown wash, over pencil. 240 × 206 mm.
PROVENANCE: J.C. Robinson; Malcolm (1895–9–15–892).
LITERATURE: JCR 439; P. Gassier, *The Drawings of Goya, the sketches, studies and individual drawings*, 1975, no. 352.

A study for an unexecuted double equestrian portrait of King Carlos IV and Queen Maria Luisa. In the autumn of 1799 Goya was appointed court painter, and during the next two years painted a series of portraits of the royal couple. The drawing probably dates from this period. A preliminary sketch for the same composition with the horses in slightly different positions is in the Prado (repr. Gassier, no. 353). The couple's costumes and the colour of the King's horse in the present study are similar to those in two large painted equestrian portraits, now in the Prado (P. Gassier and J. Wilson, *Goya his life and work*, 1971, nos 776 and 777).

Goya was the most gifted and innovative Spanish painter, draughtsman and printmaker of the eighteenth century. He balanced a successful career as a portraitist with less conventional works, notably the etched series *Los Capricos* (1797–8). His liberal sympathies constrained him to leave Spain, and he settled in Bordeaux in 1824 where he was to stay, except for two visits to Madrid, until his death in 1828.

54 Anonymous
French School mid–XVth century

A woman and child with grapes in a bower, with a bearded man

Pen and brown ink. 180 × 172 mm. An unrelated inscription concerning the fickleness of fortune below: *Hinc rerum vertigo oritur sic leta dolendis\ Sors hominum alternat variatque volubilis orbem*
PROVENANCE: J. Thane; T. Lawrence; S. Woodburn (according to a note by Robinson on the *verso*); J.C. Robinson; Malcolm (1895–9–15–589).
LITERATURE: JCR 152; Exh. London, 1894, no. 301; S. Colvin, in *Vasari Society*, III, 1907–8, no 12; H. Leporini, *Die Stilentwicklung der Handzeichnung*, 1925, no. 3; P. Lavallée, *Le dessin français*, 1948, p. 13, pl. II; Exh. London, 1972, no. 84.

The drawing was ascribed to Gentile da Fabriano by Robinson, and has since been placed with both the German and French drawings in the Department. The difficulty of attributing the drawing has perhaps led to its neglect by recent scholars, despite its high quality. Although Italianate, the refined figure style and the fashions, especially of the seated woman on the left, seem to point to France or the Burgundian empire as the country or area of origin. The detailed technique suggests the work of an illuminator of manuscripts.

The *verso* is attached to an old backing paper, on which is a damaged drawing of the *Annunciation* in pen and dark brown ink. Although stylistically reminiscent of the *recto*, it appears to be by an inferior hand.

Sunt venum heritago ordino fco beta Salutdus
Cores hominnid abdat venut qz dobelut osbau

111

55 Claude Gellée, called Claude Lorrain 1600–82

Landscape with Mercury and Argus

Pen and brown ink with brown wash and heightened with white over black chalk, on blue paper.
241 × 359 mm. Inscribed by a later hand: *Claude lorrain* and on the *verso: Claude Gillee dit le
loraine Roma 164 [. . .]* (the last digit may be 7)
PROVENANCE: S. Woodburn; H. Wellesley; Malcolm (1895–9–15–898).
LITERATURE: JCR 445; Exh. London, 1894, no. 229; Hind, 1926, no. 208; Roethlisberger 593;
Exh. Paris, 1978–9, no. 59.

The subject is taken from Ovid's *Metamorphoses* (I, 668–721): a princess of
Argos, Io, who was beloved of Jupiter, was transformed by Jupiter's jealous
wife Juno into a white heifer. Juno entrusted the beast to the hundred-eyed
giant, Argus, but Jupiter instructed his messenger, Mercury, to slay the giant,
which he did after lulling him to sleep with music.

No. 55 is one of a group of drawings executed by Claude towards the end
of the 1640s which have a pictorial finish. No related painting is known,
although the artist was to treat the same subject in a canvas of around 1660.
As a figurative draughtsman, Claude is considered less successful than in his
pure landscapes. Yet the poetic power of his work is usually enhanced by his
idiosyncratic figures, which in the present composition dominate the landscape
to an exceptional degree.

Claude, who moved from his native Lorraine to Rome at an early age,
rose from humble origins to become the most sought-after landscape painter
in Europe in the seventeenth century. Initially influenced not only by his
master, Agostino Tassi (*c.*1580–1644), but also by Paul Bril (on whom see no.
74) and by other artists working in Rome, he evolved an idealised, classically
inspired compositional formula that won him international renown. His
painted landscapes, which often include biblical or mythological figures,
depend on his sketches of the Roman *campagna*, but are usually bathed in a
clear, crepuscular light and characterised by an idyllic mood.

113

56 Claude Gellée, called Claude Lorrain 1600–82

A hut among trees

Pen and brown ink with brown wash over black chalk. 257 × 403 mm. Signed and dated, lower centre: *CL-GELE 1645*.
PROVENANCE: W. Esdaile; J.C. Robinson (L. 1433); Malcolm (1895–9–15–897).
LITERATURE: JCR 444; Exh. London, 1894, no. 227; Hind, 1926, no. 84; Roethlisberger 599.

The hut depicted appears to be a rural tavern, an unusual subject for a drawing by Claude, but one that he may have encountered in the work of Dutch artists working in Rome. Despite its focus on an informal motif, its large size, balanced composition and finished, pictorial character suggest that it was made or completed in the artist's studio. No related painting is known.

57 Claude Gellée, called Claude Lorrain 1600–82

Landscape with Paris and Oenone

Pen and brown ink with brown wash over black chalk. 202 × 297 mm. Dated below, left of centre: *1647*
PROVENANCE: R. Fisher; Malcolm (1895–9–15–899).
LITERATURE: JCR 446; Exh. London, 1894, no. 224; Hind, 1926, no. 223; Roethlisberger 660; Exh. Paris, 1978–9, no. 66.

The subject is identified by Claude in a lengthy inscription on the *verso*. Oenone, the wife of Paris, points out to him the words of undying love that he had carved into a tree: 'When Paris can live without loving his dearest Oenone, then shall the waters of the River Xanthe flow backwards to their source.' The passage forms part of Oenone's lament over Paris' infidelity with Helen. The River Xanthe is included prominently, with Troy beyond. Claude depended on the version of the tale related in the *Ravissement d'Hélène*, which was compiled, supposedly from ancient sources, by du Souhait, and published in 1634 in Paris in his edition of Homer's *Iliad*.

Dated 1647, the drawing is a preparatory study for Claude's painting of the following year, now in the Louvre, which he painted for Roger du Plessis, *seigneur* de Liancourt (1598–1674). The inscription on the *verso* further records that the canvas was delivered to Paris by the French envoy to Rome, François du Val, Marquis de Fontenay-Mareuil (*c*.1594–1665). Himself a patron of the artist, he had earlier organised for de Liancourt the commissioning of the pendant, the *Seaport with Ulysses returning Chryseis to her father* of 1644, now also in the Louvre.

116

58 Claude Gellée, called Claude Lorrain 1600–82

Pastoral landscape

Pen and brown ink with brown and grey wash, on paper tinted pink. 245 × 359 mm.
PROVENANCE: probably Paignon-Dijonval; Vicomte Morel de Vindé; T. Dimsdale; T. Lawrence
(L. 2445); W. Esdaile (L. 2617); H. Wellesley; Malcolm (1895–9–15–909).
LITERATURE: JCR 456; Exh. London, 1894, no. 226; Hind, 1926, no. 200; Roethlisberger 731;
Exh. Paris, 1978–9, no. 76.

Dated by Roethlisberger on grounds of style to the mid-1650s, the drawing is
not directly related to any other surviving composition by Claude. It was
probably made as an independent work and, like many of his paintings and
drawings, does not appear to illustrate a particular subject.

The grey wash, which is somewhat clumsily applied, may have been added
by a later hand. Similar posthumous interventions, probably dating from the
eighteenth century and made in an attempt to enhance the value of the
drawings concerned, are often found in landscape sketches by Dutch masters,
including Rembrandt.

59 Angeluccio active second half of XVIIth century

Landscape with a gate through a garden wall

Black chalk, heightened with white, on blue paper. 407 × 267 mm.
PROVENANCE: H. Wellesley; Malcolm (1895–9–15–906).
LITERATURE: JCR 453; Exh. London, 1894, no. 230; Hind 159; M. Roethlisberger, 'Drawings
around Claude [. . .] by Angeluccio', *Master Drawings*, IV, 1966, p. 383 and no. 30;
Roethlisberger, under nos 943 and 1241.

The drawing was until recently attributed to Claude Lorrain but belongs to a
distinct group of landscape studies by his assistant, known only as
Angeluccio. The artist, who was probably not French but of Italian or
Netherlandish extraction (but is included here after his master), is mentioned
briefly in L. Pascoli, *Vite de' pittori*, 1730, as a pupil of Claude's who died
young. Seventeenth-century inventories often mention his landscape
paintings, some sixteen of which have now been identified, and their
figurative staffage was sometimes provided – like some of Claude's – by two
other painters working in Rome, Michelangelo Cerquozzi (1602–60) and Jan
Miel (1599–1655).

Although Angeluccio's drawings emulate Claude in style, they have an
individual, decorative character, enhanced by his use of blue paper, that
anticipates the work of eighteenth-century French draughtsmen, including
Jean-Baptiste Oudry (1686–1755) and yet later artists like Jean-Honoré
Fragonard (1732–1806) and Hubert Robert (1733–1808). There is a slight
sketch of trees on the *verso*.

118

119

60　Robert Nanteuil 1623–78

Portrait of a man

Graphite on vellum. 145 × 110 mm (oval). Signed or inscribed below: *R. Nanteuil Faciebat Ano. 1651.*
PROVENANCE: Alliance des Arts (L. 61); J.C. Robinson; Malcolm (1895–9–15–948).
LITERATURE: JCR 496; Exh. London, 1894, no. 236a; T.H. Thomas, 'The Drawings and Pastels of Nanteuil', *Print Collectors' Quarterly*, IV, 1914, p. 336.

Nanteuil is best remembered for his portrait engravings, but he also produced a substantial *corpus* of drawings and pastels of high quality, for which he was renowned in his own day. The sitter in this sympathetic study has not been identified.

Nanteuil was born in Rheims but from 1647 spent most of his career in Paris. In 1658 he was appointed Louis XIV's *Dessinateur et graveur ordinaire du roi*, having already established his name as one of the most skilful engravers and draughtsmen in France.

120

61 Antoine Watteau 1684–1721

Study of a kitchen boy

Red chalk. 187 × 117 mm. Inscribed, lower left: *Watteau*
PROVENANCE: Colnaghi's (1869); Malcolm (1895–9–15–937).
LITERATURE: JCR 485; Exh. London, 1894, no. 239a; Parker, 1930, no. 2; Parker and Mathey, 1957, no. 254; Exh. London, 1980, no. 2.

The figure was used by Watteau in a painting of a military subject entitled *Escorte d'équipages*, which was probably executed in *c.*1710–12 and is now known only through an engraving of 1731 by Laurent Cars. Stylistically, the somewhat even use of the chalk and the careful finish argue for placing the study earlier than the painting. The drawing was etched by Boucher in Jean de Jullienne's *Figures de différents caractères, de paysages, et d'études dessinées d'après nature, par Antoine Watteau*, published in Paris in 1726–8.

Watteau is generally regarded as one of France's most fluent draughtsmen. His career began as the pupil of a local painter in his native town of Valenciennes, but from around 1703–9 he was in Paris, where he worked with Claude Gillot (1673–1722) and Claude Audran III (1658–1734). After a spell in Valenciennes, painting mostly military subjects, he returned to Paris in 1710, where he rapidly gained patrons for his *fêtes galantes* (paintings depicting actors of the *commedia dell'arte* in idealised landscape settings), including Pierre Crozat and the Swedish statesman and collector Count Tessin. He died aged thirty-seven, possibly of tuberculosis – a visit to the physician and collector Dr Meade in London in 1719–20 may have been prompted by his search for a cure.

122

62 Antoine Watteau 1684–1721

Studies of a young woman's head

Black, red and white chalk, on buff paper. 331 × 238 mm.
PROVENANCE: E.V. Utterson (L. 909); J.C. Robinson (L. 1433); Malcolm (1895–9–15–941).
LITERATURE: JCR 489; Exh. London, 1894, no. 248; Parker, 1930, no. 17; Parker and Mathey,
1957, no. 788; Exh. London, 1972, no. 263; Exh. London, 1980, no. 19 (with further literature);
Exh. London, 1984, no. 124.

Watteau made several comparable studies of heads, adding them to the stock
of drawings that he used for his paintings. A study that was probably made
at the same sitting and from the same model is in a private collection (Parker
and Mathey, 783), and another closely comparable drawing is now in the
Museum of Fine Arts in Boston (Forsyth Wickes collection, *ibid.*, no. 786),
but no painting related to the present sheet is known.

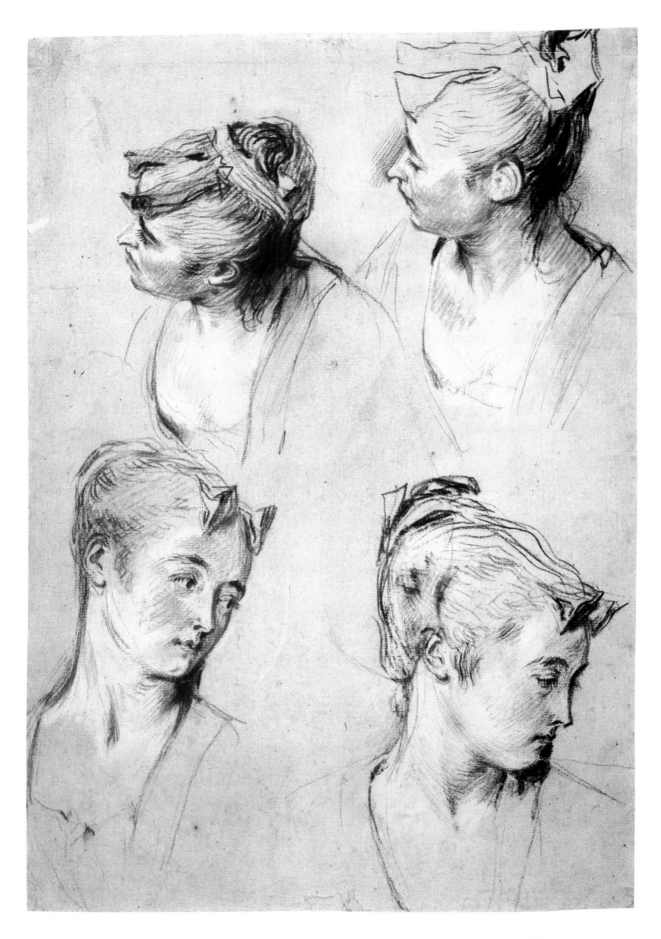

63 François Boucher 1703–70

Pastoral composition, with two young lovers

Black chalk, heightened with white and pale yellow. 230 × 297 mm.
PROVENANCE: J.C. Robinson; Malcolm (1895–9–15–955).
LITERATURE: JCR 502; A. Ananoff, *François Boucher*, 1976, I, p. 376, under no. 260,3;
Exh. Tokyo and Kumamoto, 1982, *François Boucher*, no. 101.

One of a pair of drawings of amorous pastoral subjects from Malcolm's collection, presumably the ones recorded in his manuscript *Memorandum of prices* as having been purchased on 21 May 1866 from J.C. Robinson, who was then probably acting as Malcolm's agent (see the Introduction, n. 29). Both drawings were engraved by G.F. Schmidt (1712–75), the present one with the title *Les amours pastorales*, and the disciplined drawing style suggests that Boucher intended them as models for prints.

Boucher was one of the most successful, versatile and prolific painters of eighteenth-century France. His decorative style typifies the Rococo and was primarily based on his thorough aquaintance with paintings and sketches by Watteau, after whose drawings he made etchings for Jean de Jullienne's *Figures de différents caractères* as a young man (see under no. 61). He became drawing-master to Louis XVI's mistress, Madame de Pompadour, whom he advised on all her artistic projects, and in 1765 succeeded Carle Vanloo as Director of the Académie Royale and *premier peintre du roi*.

64 After Stefan Lochner c.1410–51

The Virgin adoring the infant Christ

Pen and black ink. 129 × 172 mm.
PROVENANCE: F. Fagel; J.C. Robinson; Malcolm (1895–9–15–1007).
LITERATURE: JCR 549; Exh. London, 1894, no. 259; Exh. London, 1988, no. 9; Rowlands 1 (with
further literature); Exh. Cologne, Wallraf-Richartz-Museum, *Stefan Lochner, Meister zu Köln*,
1993, no. 90.

The drawing is an early copy after Stefan Lochner's painting of the *Adoration of the Child* now in the Alte Pinakothek, Munich (inv. no. 13169). The style resembles the underdrawings in Lochner's paintings, recently made visible through infra-red reflectography, and the drawing may therefore have been made in Lochner's own studio.

The painting copied in the drawing is on the left wing of an altarpiece, with the *Crucifixion* on the reverse; the other wing, which is dated 1445, represents the *Presentation of Christ in the Temple* and the *Stigmatisation of St Francis* and is now in the Museu Calouste Gulbenkian, Lisbon (inv. no. 272). Another copy, showing the Virgin only, is in the École des Beaux-Arts, Paris (Masson Collection, no. 128).

Information concerning Lochner is scarce. He is chiefly documented in Cologne, and was probably responsible for an altarpiece of the *Adoration of the Magi*, now in the town's cathedral.

65   Martin Schongauer   *c*.1450–91

An angel

Pen and brown ink. 184 × 100 mm.
PROVENANCE: J.C. Robinson; Malcolm (1895–9–15–961*).
LITERATURE: JCR 508; Exh. London, 1894, no. 262(b); Rowlands 16 (with further literature);
Exh. Colmar, Musée d'Unterlinden, *Le Beau Martin*, 1991, no. D35.

The drawing is probably a late work, contemporary with Schongauer's
frescoes of the *Last Judgment* in the Münster at Breisach, where he was
recorded as a citizen on 15 June 1489. There is an outline sketch of a female
figure on the *verso*. When acquired by Malcolm the drawing was attached
with a blank strip of paper to a second, similar study (with which it is still
mounted) that shows a *Man holding a book* (Rowlands 17). Another, perhaps
related drawing of an *Angel* was recently in a private collection (repr. Exh.
London, British Museum and elsewhere, *German Drawings from a Private
Collection*, by J. Rowlands, 1984, no. 7).

    Martin Schongauer, the son of a goldsmith, is considered the most
significant German painter and engraver before Dürer. He was probably born
in Colmar, where he established a workshop in or before 1471. Towards the
end of his life he settled in Breisach, where he died in 1491.

66 Albrecht Dürer 1471–1528

View of the castle at Trent

Pen and black ink with watercolour and light touches of white bodycolour. 196 × 250 mm.
Inscribed by the artist, upper right: *trint*
PROVENANCE: A.F. Andréossy; T. Lawrence (L. 2445); S. Woodburn; C. Goodrich; Malcolm
(1895-9-15-975).
LITERATURE: JCR 522; Exh. London, 1894, no. 268; Exh. London, 1988, no. 39; Rowlands 124
(with further literature).

This well-preserved watercolour is one of two surviving views by Dürer of
the castle at Trent; the other, taken from the north, is now in the Kunsthalle
in Bremen (inv. no. 10). They were probably made in the spring of 1495 on
the return journey of Dürer's first visit to Italy. Other contemporary
watercolour landscapes by him are known including two made near Trent, the
Cambra Valley near Segonzano (Ashmolean Museum, Oxford, P.284) and the
Castle at Segonzano (Berlin, Kupferstichkabinett, KdZ.24622).

Albrecht Dürer, the most celebrated German artist, was born in
Nuremberg, the son of a goldsmith. He studied under his father and with
Michel Wolgemut (1434–1519). After travelling in northern Germany and
perhaps also the Netherlands, he worked in Basle (1492-4) and visited
northern Italy (1494-5). Already employed by Friedrich the Wise, Duke of
Saxony, in the mid-1490s, his international reputation was secured by his
series of woodcut illustrations to the *Apocalypse*, published in 1498. Widely
admired as a remarkable printmaker and draughtsman, his style was enriched
by a second visit to Italy (1505-7). After his return to Nuremberg in 1507 he
worked on several important paintings and further print series, including the
Engraved Passion (1507-13) and three woodcut series of 1511, the *Life of the
Virgin*, the *Great Passion* and the *Little Passion*. From 1510 he was employed
by the Holy Roman Emperors, Maximilian I – for whom he produced the
woodcut of the *Triumphal arch* (1515-17) and was involved, with Hans
Burgkmair, in the *Triumphal procession* (1516-19) – and his successor,
Charles V. In 1519 the artist visited Switzerland, and in 1520 journeyed to
the Netherlands, where he met Lucas van Leyden.

67 Albrecht Dürer 1471–1528

A woman of Nuremberg dressed for church

Drawn with the tip of the brush and with watercolour. 316 × 171 mm. Inscribed by the artist, above: *1500 AD* [in mon.] *Ein Nörmergerin / as man zu kirchen gatt* ('a Nuremberg woman as one goes to church').
PROVENANCE: E. Knight; S. Woodburn; W. Russell; J.(?) Whitehead; Malcolm (1895–9–15–973).
LITERATURE: JCR 520; Exh. London, 1894, no. 271; Exh. London, 1984, no. 46; Exh. London, 1988, no. 46; Rowlands 145 (with further literature).

The woman's features resemble those of Dürer's wife, Agnes Frey, whom he married in 1494. She wears a headdress known as a *Stürz*, made of starched linen arranged over a frame.

As was already pointed out by Robinson, Dürer employed the figure, in reverse, in his woodcut of the *Betrothal of the Virgin* (Bartsch 82) from the set of the *Life of the Virgin* published in 1511. Dürer made several other costume studies around the turn of the century, including another version of the present drawing, now in the Albertina, Vienna (inv. no. 3060.D.45). In the latter, the figure is rendered in greater detail, and the more spontaneous drawing in the British Museum may have served as a preliminary study for it.

A sixteenth-century copy of no. 67 is also in the British Museum (Rowlands, Appendix II, no. 15).

33

68 Albrecht Dürer 1471–1528

Head of a woman

Silverpoint, heightened with white, on paper prepared with a pink ground. 218 × 181 mm.
PROVENANCE: E. Piot; J.C. Robinson; Malcolm (1895–9–15–978).
LITERATURE: JCR 525; Exh. London, 1894, no. 273; Rowlands 169 (with further literature).

The drawing has been variously dated by Dürer specialists and its authorship
occasionally questioned. It may have been made in Italy at the same time as
the *Feast of the rosary* altarpiece of 1506 now in the National Gallery in
Prague. Dürer's preparatory studies for the painting, made with the brush,
are comparable, especially the *Head of an angel* now in the Albertina,
Vienna, which is dated 1506 (inv. no. 30099.D.78). In the present drawing,
the influence of Italian art is strongly evident, both in the technique that
Dürer employed and in the classical poise and ideal features of the head.

69 Hans Baldung, called Grien 1484/5–1545

The Virgin and child seated on a bank

Pen and black and brown ink. 164 × 168 mm. Inscribed below with a false Dürer monogram: *AD*
PROVENANCE: E. Desperet (L. 721); Malcolm (1895–9–15–967).
LITERATURE: JCR 514; Rowlands 58 (with further literature).

Although frequently ascribed in the past to Dürer, whose style is closely
emulated here, the drawing has now been returned to Hans Baldung,
following the attribution proposed by J.C. Robinson in the Malcolm catalogue.
The purpose of the drawing is unknown, but it would certainly be an early
work by Baldung, datable to the first years of the sixteenth century.

Nothing is recorded of Baldung's training, although he probably worked
with Dürer in Nuremberg from 1503 until *c*.1507. Thereafter he was principally based in Strasburg. A prolific designer of prints, Baldung was a highly
inventive and original artist, the expressive character of whose work may
have been stimulated by Mathis Grünewald (*c*.1480 or *c*.1470/75–1528), whose
altarpiece with the *Crucifixion* at Isenheim was completed in around 1515.

70 Hans Holbein the Younger 1497/8–1543

A wild man brandishing an uprooted tree-trunk

Pen and black ink with grey, brown and blue wash. 321 × 215 mm.
PROVENANCE: F. Fagel; T. Philipe; Malcolm (1895–9–15–992).
LITERATURE: JCR 536; Exh. London, 1894, no. 288; P. Ganz, *Die Handzeichnungen Hans Holbein d.J. Kritischer Katalog*, 1912–37, no. 200; Exh. London, 1984, no. 58; Exh. London, 1988, no. 195; Rowlands 316 (with further literature).

The drawing style, with its simplified outlines, is typical for a design for stained glass. The design was probably intended for a window in the meeting-place, or *Ehrengesellschafthaus*, of the civic society 'Zur Hären' based in Klein Basel, the part of the town north of the Rhine. The society employed the image of the wild man with an uprooted tree-trunk as its emblem. Its membership originally consisted of fishermen and hunters, but later also included members of the aristocracy.

The window itself is no longer known, but may have been the 'Vitrau peint. Armoirie de la société de la Hären au petit Basle, un homme sauvage', which was recorded in 1841 in the stock of a Basel dealer, Johann Heinrich Speyr. What appears to be an early copy of the drawing is now in the Kupferstichkabinett, Berlin (KdZ. 3091).

Holbein was one of the most versatile German artists to emerge after the maturity of Dürer. Active as a painter and draughtsman, he also produced designs for prints, metalwork, stained glass and jewellery. He was born in Augsburg, where he received instruction from his father, Hans Holbein the Elder. From 1515 he was based in Basel, but worked in England from 1526–8 and from 1532 until his death in 1543.

137

71 School of
Rogier van der Weyden *c.*1399–1464

A religious procession

Pen and brown ink over traces of black chalk. 292 × 531 mm.
PROVENANCE: T. Lawrence (according to JCR); J.C. Robinson (L. 1433); Malcolm (1895–9–15–1001).
LITERATURE: JCR 543; Exh. London, 1894, no. 303; Popham, 1932, p. 56, no. 6; M. Sonkes, *Dessins du XVe siècle*, 1969, no. C41 (with further literature); Exh. London, 1972, no. 103.

In the drawing's present condition (it may have been cut on the right), the procession is led by the three priests on the platform on the right, followed by eight choristers and an elderly cleric on the steps. The officiating priest, holding the *ciborium*, heads the next group, accompanied by a deacon and sub-deacon, with a prominent figure behind in a hat and robes. The sequence of five figures behind him is interrupted by a break in the drawing, where the last quarter of the composition is attached on a separate piece of paper. Here the procession is seen to emerge from a gate, where a beggar receives alms, his dog beside him holding a bowl.

The strongly individualised characterisations may be paralleled in the work of Rogier, to whom the drawing was attributed in the mid-nineteenth century. The quality is impressive and reminiscent of a drawing in the Metropolitan Museum of Art in New York (Robert Lehman Collection) which represents, in the vein of Hieronymus Bosch, men shovelling three-legged stools (the *Stool-scoopers* or *Scupstoel*). Although a *genre* scene, this is probably by the same hand, being in the same technique and with figures of comparable character. Both drawings appear to be by an able member of Rogier's workshop or by some other follower. No work related to the present composition is known, but the drawing, which may date from before Rogier's visit to Italy in 1449-50, probably depends on a lost decorative scheme designed by the master.

Rogier van der Weyden, the son of a sculptor, became one of the most celebrated artists of the Burgundian Netherlands. Having trained and worked in his native Tournai, he was town painter in Brussels, which had come under the sway of Duke Philip the Good of Burgundy's luxurious court.

72 Anonymous
Netherlandish School XV–XVIth century

The Tree of Jesse

Pen and dark brown ink, heightened with white, on paper with a blue preparation.
266 × 343 mm. Inscribed *xxxij* on the canopy.
PROVENANCE: Sibthorpe; J.C. Robinson; Malcolm (1895–9–15–1005).
LITERATURE: JCR 547; Exh. London, 1894, no. 304; Popham, 1932, p. 80, no. 67.

The drawing depicts the genealogical tree of Christ, based on Isaiah's prophecy that a Messiah would be born to the family of Jesse, the father of King David. Jesse is depicted asleep in a *baldacchino* on a level with other prophets or patriarchs. Above, immediately to the left of the canopy, is David playing the harp, with the Virgin and child at the top centre, surrounded by others of the twelve Kings of Judah.

The composition has elements in common with three other works of art: an engraving by the Master of the Banderoles (Lehrs 80); an illuminated Bible of around 1440–50 in the British Library (Add. MS 15254); and a painting of 1518 by the so-called Master Jean in the Antwerp Museum. The first of these is the closest, although it shows twelve instead of four patriarchs and prophets in the lower register, and the kings are arranged differently. This suggests that all these works are derived from a common prototype, now unknown, one that must have been made by the mid-fifteenth century. In addition, a copy of the present composition, but in reverse, was on the Amsterdam art market in 1929.

Although dependent on a fifteenth-century model, the technique of drawing on a coloured surface points to a later date, perhaps in the first half of the sixteenth century.

140

73   Johan Wierix   1549–1618 or later

Whole-length portrait of a woman

Pen and brown ink on vellum. 241 × 170 mm. Signed to left: *Johan. W.F.1584* and inscribed, upper right: *A° Aetat[. . .]*
PROVENANCE: James West; Colnaghi's (1888); Malcolm (1895–9–15–1352).
LITERATURE: Exh. London, 1894, no. 321; Popham, 1932, p. 196, no. 30.

The drawing was thought to represent the wife of Jean Pilier, of whom there is an engraving by Wierix (M. Mauquoy-Hendrickx, *Les estampes des Wierix*, 1982, no. 1905). However, the print is dated 1605 and gives the sitter's age as twenty-one, which would mean that she was born in 1584, the year that this drawing was made. The woman is luxuriantly attired, holding a fan and a handkerchief and with a book attached to her waist by a cord.

Weirix frequently made highly finished drawings on vellum, often in the form of series of biblical illustrations. Only a few are on a comparable scale to the present sheet, an extraordinary technical *tour-de-force* made at the same time as some of Hendrick Goltzius' most elaborate *penwerken*. Clearly intended as an independent work of art, the original function of such a drawing is no longer known. It was acquired by Malcolm from Colnaghi's in 1888 for £100, an exceptionally high sum.

The draughtsman was a member of a family of skilled but prolific engravers, who concentrated on providing illustrations to the Antwerp publishers Christopher Plantin and Philips Galle.

74 Paul Bril 1554–1626

Trees at the edge of a pool

Pen and brown ink with brown and grey wash. 158 × 225 mm. Signed, lower left: *Pa. Bril 1609
In. Romae*
PROVENANCE: Wells of Redleaf; J.C. Robinson; Malcolm (1895–9–15–1029).
LITERATURE: JCR 571; Exh. London, 1894, no. 340; Popham, 1932, pp. 137–8, no. 4; Exh.
London, National Gallery, *Dutch Landscape: the early years*, 1986, no. 3.

A characteristic late drawing by Bril, in which the expansive, flat landscape
with counterpoised groups of trees anticipates the compositions of Claude
Lorrain (see nos 55–8). The signature and the high degree of finish, also seen
in many other drawings by Bril, suggest that it was intended as an
independent work of art in its own right, rather than as a study for a
painting or a print.

Bril left the Netherlands in around 1574 and settled in Rome where his
brother, the artist Matthijs Bril (1550–83), was also established. They worked
as a team specialising in landscape, most conspicuously in the *Torre dei Venti*
in the Vatican. Paul continued to work independently after his brother's death
in 1583. Before around 1600, his style remained strongly Mannerist in
flavour, his compositions dominated by rocky scenery that is indebted to
Patenir and Bruegel; but his later landscapes, like that shown here, have a
more idyllic mood.

75 Hendrick Goltzius 1558–1617

Self-portrait

Silverpoint on prepared yellow surface on vellum. 145 × 103 mm. Inscribed top left with the artist's monogram.

PROVENANCE: J. de Vries sale, 1738; V. Röver (L. *Suppl.*, 2984a-c, *verso*); J. Goll van Franckenstein; J.G. Verstolk van Soelen; G. Leembruggen; Malcolm (1895–9–15–1020).

LITERATURE: JCR 562; Exh. London, 1894, no. 325a; Popham, 1932, p. 162, no. 10; E.K.J. Reznicek, *Die Zeichnungen von Hendrick Goltzius*, 1961, no. 254; Exh. London, 1972, no. 161; Exh. London, 1974, no. 13.

The drawing, though recorded as a self-portrait in 1739 when in the Röver collection, was considered in the nineteenth century to be a portrait of Goltzius' stepson, the engraver Jacob Matham. Acquired as such by Malcolm, the earlier identification of the artist is, however, correct, as may be judged from Goltzius' other self-portraits, in particular an elaborate chalk drawing now in Stockholm (Reznicek 255). The present work is among the most highly finished of all Goltzius' drawings, although it may have been made in an informal sketchbook, as the *verso* contains a slight sketch of a camel. This is stylistically comparable to a sketchbook page of animal studies in silverpoint now in Munich, on which another camel appears (Reznicek 417). The artist created something of a revival in the medium of silverpoint, inspired by the example of artists of the Renaissance, including Dürer in particular.

Goltzius, a leading figure in late sixteenth-century Netherlandish art, was a pupil of the humanist and engraver Dirck Volckertsz. Coornhert, and settled in Haarlem in 1576–7. He concentrated exclusively on drawing and print-making until around 1600, achieving international renown; when he travelled to Italy in 1590–91, he went *incognito* to avoid incurring unwelcome obligations. In 1600 he stopped engraving and became a full-time painter, continuing with drawing as a peripheral activity. Jacob de Gheyn (see nos 76–7) was one of his pupils.

76 Jacob de Gheyn the Younger 1565–1629

Allegory on the equality of all mankind in death

Pen and brown ink with brown wash and grey wash, indented for transfer; the child drawn on a separate piece of paper that has been inserted. 459 × 349 mm. Signed lower left: *DGheyn in. 1599* and extensively inscribed.
PROVENANCE: A. Devéria; J.C. Robinson; Malcolm (1895–9–15–1031).
LITERATURE: JCR 573; Exh. London, 1894, no. 331; Popham, 1932, p. 156, no. 1; I.Q. van Regteren Altena, *Jacques de Gheyn. Three Generations*, 1983, no. 204; Exh. Rotterdam, Museum Boymans-van Beuningen, *Jacques de Gheyn II als tekenaar*, 1985–6, no. 13 (with further literature).

The drawing is a full-size preparatory study, in reverse, for an engraving (Hollstein 98). Its iconography is derived from the inscriptions, most of them written on the drawing in the cursive script of the young scholastic prodigy Hugo Grotius (1583–1645). The overriding theme is announced around the top of the *baldacchino*: 'Death makes the sceptre and the spade equal' (*MORS SCEPTRA LIGONIBVS AEQVAT*). The related print in its second state bears above a further title that is not seen in the drawing: 'The Soul's edifying Bridle of the Flesh' (*S'Geests Stichtigen Vleesch-Breydel*). Death is therefore seen as the equaliser of men of all classes and its contemplation a spur to abstinence from sins of the flesh.

An owl and a lamp, symbols respectively of death and of human life, stand on the rim above. To either side, roundels depict the *Fall of Man* and the *Crucifixion*, explained in the inscriptions as images of the two 'trees' (the Tree of Life and the cross) at which death and the devil first triumphed and were then defeated. The quatrain below the central fictive painting of the *Last Judgment* urges the beholder to be prepared for death. Figures of a peasant and an Emperor flank the scene, with between them a traditional emblem of the transience of human life, the child blowing soap-bubbles (*HOMO BVLLA*, 'Man is [as] a soap-bubble'). The lines on his throne emphasize the theme: 'Who shall escape?'; 'One night awaits everyone'; 'The road of death must be trodden once'; 'Death alone sees how weak is the body of man'; 'Think of Death'. The three quatrains below further stress the equality of all men in death.

De Gheyn was a prolific designer of prints, engraving many of the plates himself. A pupil of Hendrick Goltzius in Haarlem, his imagery is similarly varied and sophisticated, although Goltzius' leanings were towards Roman Catholicism while de Gheyn, as here, tends to sympathise with Calvinist ideology. He was later active in Amsterdam, Leiden, and The Hague. In the latter city he found employment at court, including work for the Stadholder, Prince Maurits of Orange.

77 Jacob de Gheyn the Younger 1565–1629

Two studies of a nude woman holding a mirror

Silverpoint on paper prepared with a cream surface, with some pen and brown ink.
335 × 220 mm.
PROVENANCE: J. Reynolds (L. 2364 *verso*); T. Lawrence (L. 2445); J.C. Robinson (L. 1433,
erased); Malcolm (1895–9–15–979).
LITERATURE: Exh. London, Burlington Fine Arts Club, *Albert Dürer and Lucas van Leyden*,
1869, no. 10; JCR 526; K.T. Parker, *Guide to the Woodcuts, Drawings and Engravings of
Albrecht Dürer [. . .]*, 1928, p. 32, no. 297; J.K. Rowlands, *Master Drawings*, X, 1972, pp. 284–6;
Exh. BM, *Gainsborough and Reynolds in the British Museum*, 1978, p. 69 and no. 269; K.G.
Boon, *The Netherlandish and German Drawings [. . .] Frits Lugt Collection*, 1992, I, p. 152 (with
further literature).

Attributed to Albrecht Dürer when acquired by Malcolm, the modern
consensus is that the drawing is probably by Jacques de Gheyn, as was first
proposed by K.T. Parker. De Gheyn, like his master Hendrick Goltzius,
emulated the techniques and styles of Dürer and other Renaissance masters
(for a time the present drawing was ascribed to Lucas van Leyden). The
model is observed from two different angles, rather as though from a statue,
an idea also suggested by the sheen of the figure on the right. She holds a
mirror and may therefore have been intended as an allegorical representation
of Prudence. Indeed, the figure was employed by the former owner of the
drawing, Joshua Reynolds, for his depiction of Prudence in his stained glass
design for the window of New College, Oxford.

78 Peter Paul Rubens 1577–1640

A man leading a horse
after Polidoro da Caravaggio 1499/1500–1543?

Brush drawing in brown with some pen and brown ink, heightened with white. 427 × 235 mm.
PROVENANCE: P.H. Lankrink (L. 2090 and *Suppl.*); J.C. Robinson; Malcolm (1895–9–15–653).
LITERATURE: JCR 212; Hind, II, 1923, p. 20, no. 47; Pouncey and Gere 225; M. Jaffé, *Rubens and Italy*, 1977, p. 48; Exh. BM, *Rubens. Drawings and Sketches*, 1977, no. 32.

From 1600 to 1608 Rubens was in Italy, where he studied and copied the Antique as well as works by Italian Renaissance masters. In the present drawing he followed in his own style part of a fresco decoration by Raphael's pupil Polidoro da Caravaggio: the painted frieze on the façade of the Palazzo Milesi in the Via della Maschera d'Oro in Rome, now in a ruinous condition but known through engravings and other early copies. When owned by Malcolm, the drawing was considered to be by Polidoro himself; Rubens was much inspired by the Italian painter's heroic figure style, and copies after other sections of the same frieze have been attributed to him.

Rubens was the most successful and influential painter of the Flemish Baroque. After his return to Antwerp from Italy, where he had already found ready employment, he worked for many of the royal houses of western Europe, most notably for Charles I, Louis XIII, Maria dei Medici and Philip IV.

151

79 Peter Paul Rubens 1577–1640

The Battle of the Standard

Black chalk with touches of red chalk, with brown wash. 415 × 522 mm. Inscribed top left by the artist (now hardly decipherable): *guarda [. . .] Mediana [?] far si che colui [. . .] il Colpo si alsi su piedi sopra le staffe [. . .] avvicinare gli nemici*, and lower right, by a later hand: *PP. Rubens*
PROVENANCE: P.H. Lankrink (L. 2090 and *Suppl.*); T. Dimsdale (according to Hind); T. Lawrence (L. 2445); J.C. Robinson (L. 1433); Malcolm (1895-9-15-1044).
LITERATURE: JCR 585; Exh. London, 1894, no. 347; Hind, II, 1923, p. 12, no. 21; G. Glück and F.M. Haberditzl, *Die Handzeichnungen von Peter Paul Rubens*, 1928, no. 8; M. Jaffé, *Rubens and Italy*, 1977, pp. 30 and 71; Exh. BM, *Rubens. Drawings and Sketches*, 1977, no. 22.

In this tumultuous scene, Rubens reworked motifs from Leonardo da Vinci's *Battle of Anghiari* into an invention of his own. Most of the figures appear so wholly Leonardesque in facial type and expression that Rubens may have based them on a now lost drawing that recorded a stage in the development of Leonardo's composition. Yet the horse to the left appears entirely Rubensian, and may be compared with that in a drawing of a *Man in armour on horseback* of 1603 (now in the Louvre; see J.S. Held, *Rubens. Selected Drawings*, 1986, no. 26). The present sheet may date from slightly later, perhaps shortly before Rubens returned to Antwerp from Italy late in 1608.

The *Battle of Anghiari*, intended as a fresco in the Palazzo Vecchio in Florence, was never completed, and Rubens can only have known it through early copies based on the cartoon (now lost) and through Leonardo's own preparatory drawings. The composition appealed strongly to Rubens, who drew an elaborate, if not entirely accurate, reconstruction of it, now in the Louvre (Held, *op. cit.*, no. 49), that was later engraved by Gerard Edelinck (1640–1707). Echoes of Leonardo's design appear in many of Rubens' hunting and battle scenes.

153

80 Anthony van Dyck 1599–1641

Portrait of Sebastian Vrancx (1573–1647)

Black chalk. 257 × 188 mm. Inscribed in brown ink: *SEBAST. FRANCK.*
PROVENANCE: J. de Vos; E. Cheney; Malcolm (1895–9–15–1073).
LITERATURE: Exh. London, 1894, no. 361; Hind, II, 1923, p. 61, no. 34; H. Vey, *Die Zeichnungen Anton van Dycks*, 1962, no. 250 (with further literature); Exh. London, 1974, no. 98.

The sitter, a pupil with Rubens of Adam van Noort, was a successful painter who specialised in battle-pieces and scenes of brigandry set in landscapes.

The drawing is one of many surviving preparatory studies for the series of engraved portraits published by Van Dyck in his *Iconography*. This series, which grew out of a set of eighteen etchings made by van Dyck in the late 1620s, portrayed many of his most distinguished contemporaries, and was issued in three broad groups: princes and military commanders; statesmen and philosophers; and artists and collectors. Van Dyck's initial group of eighteen etchings, mostly of artists, was expanded into a compendium of some 100 prints, a project he undertook, in all probability, with the encouragement of the Antwerp publisher, Martinus van den Enden.

The present drawing was engraved for the series by Schelte à Bolswert, who may also have made use of a related sketch in oils by van Dyck (Buccleuch collection). A further drawing, possibly by van Dyck or a member of his studio, is in the Teylers Museum in Haarlem. Most of the work on the series was done in Antwerp between 1627 and the mid-1630s, but the project was not completed in van Dyck's lifetime. It was first published as a set soon after his death in 1641.

Van Dyck was the most gifted pupil of Rubens (see nos 78–9), and particularly sought after for his portraits. He worked mostly in Antwerp (to 1620; from 1627–32 and 1634–5), Italy (1621–7) and London (1620–21; 1632–4 and 1635–41).

SEBAST FRANCK.

81 Jacob Jordaens 1593–1678

Veritas Dei

Black and red chalk, with brown wash and watercolour, heightened with white. 346 × 267 mm.
Inscribed in pen and brown ink, lower right: *J. Jordaens* and with the title, upper left, on the
book: *VERITAS DEI.* Below, on the fictive plinth, is the reference: *GAL.6.CAP*
PROVENANCE: J.C. Robinson; Malcolm (1895–9–15–1075).
LITERATURE: JCR 615; Exh. London, 1894, no. 362; Hind, II, 1923, p. 110, no. 2; R.-A. d'Hulst,
Jordaens Drawings, I, 1974, no. A226 (with further literature).

The composition is an allegory illustrating *Galatians*, VI, viii: 'For he that
soweth to his flesh shall of the flesh reap corruption; but he that soweth to
the Spirit shall of the Spirit reap life everlasting.' A preacher in a pulpit, who
is presumably St Paul, addresses the figures below, including Charity with
her children beside an old woman with a cross and rosary, Innocence (the
child with the lamb) and a sinner threatened by Envy (with the vipers),
Hypocrisy (with a mask) and another Vice. The preacher indicates the
personification of the Truth of God (*Veritas Dei*), who holds a book, a chalice
and above whom the Holy Spirit hovers (the dove).

The drawing is one of four by Jordaens related to the same composition,
which was probably intended for a tapestry (the others are in Vienna and two
private collections). A set depicting the *Acts of the Apostles* was listed in the
1679 inventory of the possessions of a tapestry dealer, Michiel Wauters, and
the design may have been used in that series. A copy of the present drawing
is in the Musée des Beaux-Arts et d'Archéologie, Rennes.

The artist, who produced numerous coloured tapestry designs in the same
medium, was the leading painter in Antwerp after the death of Rubens –
whose style he emulated – in 1640. Both had been trained in the workshop of
Adam van Noort, whose daughter Jordaens married in 1616.

157

82 Jan van Goyen 1596–1656

Cottages amid trees and a ruin on the banks of a river

Black chalk with brown and grey wash. 200 × 315 mm. Signed and dated lower left: *VG* [in monogram] *1651*
PROVENANCE: Malcolm (1895–9–15–1165).
LITERATURE: Exh. London, 1894, no. 367b; Hind, III, 1926, p. 103, no. 4; H.–U. Beck, *Jan van Goyen 1596–1656: ein Oeuvreverzeichnis*, 1972, I, no. 283.

Large numbers of drawings by Jan van Goyen survive from towards the end of his life, many of them dated in the same year, 1651, as the present example. In his late drawings he seems to have preferred to concentrate on producing finished, marketable drawings rather than slight sketches of the type he had often made before.

A specialist in landscape painting and drawing, van Goyen also produced some *genre* scenes at the start of his career, still influenced by his last teacher, Esaias van de Velde. He was at first based in his native town, Haarlem, but settled in The Hague in around 1632. There he became head of the artists' guild in 1638 and 1640, and he painted a large view of The Hague for the burgomaster's room in the town hall, for which he received 650 guilders, a substantial sum. His daughter Margaretha married the *genre* painter Jan Steen in 1649.

159

83 Pieter Jansz. Saenredam 1597–1665

The choir and high altar of the St Janskerk, 's-Hertogenbosch

Pen and brown ink with black chalk and watercolour. 408 × 320 mm. Inscribed by the artist, lower left: *de St Jans, ofte grote, kerk, in sHartogenbosch, in brabant, van mij P'. Saenredam 1632 den 1 Julij aldus naer t'leeven geteekent.*
PROVENANCE: J.C. Robinson; Malcolm (1895-9-15-1300).
LITERATURE: JCR 825; Exh. London, 1894, no. 444; Hind, IV, 1931, p. 45, no. 1; Exh. Utrecht, Centraal Museum, *Catalogue raisonné of the works of P.J. Saenredam . . .*, 1961, no. 95, fig. 97 (with previous literature); G. Schwarz and M.J. Bock, *Pieter Saenredam*, 1989, cat. 95, fig. 89; Exh. 's-Hertogenbosch, Noordbrabants Museum, *In Buscoducis 1450 1629*, ed. A.M. Koldeweij, 1990, no. 8.

When drawn by Saenredam on 1 July 1632, almost three years after 's-Hertogenbosch had fallen into Protestant hands under Frederick Henry of Orange, the town's main church still retained its Roman Catholic appearance. The drawing shows the altar of 1617–20, designed by Hans van Mildert, still in place, as well as the statues of the apostles, carved in Antwerp in 1620, which remained *in situ* until two years later, in 1634. Also visible are the tomb of Bishop Masius on the north side of the choir and the coats-of-arms behind the altar, placed there to commemorate the funeral masses said in the church for Philip II in 1598 and Albert of Austria in 1621. A related painting by Saenredam, executed in 1646, is now in the National Gallery of Art in Washington (Schwarz and Bock, *op. cit.*, cat. 94, fig. 215). This also shows the high altar, but substitutes an *Adoration of the Shepherds* by Abraham Bloemaert for the altarpiece of the *Trinity* originally supplied by Bloemaert for the church in 1615, but which was removed in 1629. The *Adoration*, which is now in the Louvre, was painted in 1612 for the Poor Clares in the *Klarissenklooster*, and was still there when Saenredam made his painting. A second drawing of the interior of the same church, dated two days later, which depicts the rood screen (now in the Victoria and Albert Museum), is also in the British Museum (Hind 2, 1883-7-14-102).

Pieter Saenredam specialised in topographical paintings, drawings and etchings, mostly of church interiors. He was born at Assendelft, the son of the engraver Jan Saenredam, but lived for the most part in Haarlem, though he travelled to many centres in the Dutch Republic. In 1636 he made numerous studies of the churches in Utrecht, and drawings made in other cities are dated at various times in the 1630s and 1640s.

ALBERTO AUSTRIACO

16 O 21

PATRI PATRIÆ
SILVA = DVCIS.
DICAT CONSECRAT

161

84 Rembrandt 1606–69

Christ walking on the waves

Pen and brown ink. 165 × 265 mm.
PROVENANCE: Anon. collection TW (L. 2468; Thomas Williams of Somers Town?); J.C.
Robinson (L. 1433); Malcolm (1895–9–15–1262).
LITERATURE: JCR 790; Exh. London, 1894, no. 382; Hind, I, 1915, p. 32, no. 72; Benesch 70;
Exh. London, 1992, no. 7 (with further literature); P. Schatborn, *Oud Holland*, CVIII, 1994,
p. 21; J. Giltaij, *Simiolus*, XXIII, 1995, p. 96, fig. 2.

The subject is from Matthew, XIV, 29–31: St Peter attempts to walk with
Christ on the Sea of Galilee. Only two other apostles are depicted, the one
leaving the boat possibly being St Peter at an earlier moment.

As with many of Rembrandt's drawings, the attribution is not wholly
certain. No related painting or print is known, although the drawing
conforms in style with his work of the early 1630s. The variety of the
penwork, from the thin hatching lines in Christ's robe to the boldly expressed
prow of the boat, seems typical for Rembrandt, as does the strongly
characterised figure of St Peter kneeling.

Rembrandt Harmensz. van Rijn, the most celebrated artist of the Dutch
school, was born in Leiden and became a pupil of Pieter Lastman in
Amsterdam, where he settled in around 1631. His chief success was as a
portrait painter, but he also treated religious and mythological subjects,
everyday *genre* scenes, and landscape. His achievements as a painter,
printmaker and draughtsman were equally distinguished, and are all noted for
their originality in technique and their realistic approach to iconography.

85 Rembrandt 1606–69

A young woman sleeping (Hendrickje Stoffels)

Drawn with the brush in brown wash, with some white bodycolour. 246 × 203 mm.
PROVENANCE: Andrew James; Malcolm (1895–9–15–1279).
LITERATURE: JCR 807; Exh. London, 1894, no. 375; Hind, I, 1915, p. 39, no. 97; Benesch 1103;
Exh. London, 1992, no. 58 (with further literature).

This study, drawn entirely with the brush, is in an unusual technique for
Rembrandt, who generally employed the pen or chalk to define the forms in
his drawings. In style it is comparable to his painting of Hendrickje Stoffels
in the National Gallery in London, the *Woman bathing in a stream* (N.G.
54). In the painting, which is dated 1654, she wears a similar, loose-fitting
garment and the two works may date from the same period.

In 1654 Hendrickje Stoffels (*c.*1626–63), who had entered the artist's
household by 1649, gave birth to their daughter Cornelia.

86 Rembrandt 1606–69

Four orientals seated under a tree

Pen and brown ink with brown and grey wash, touched with white and with some scraping-out, on oriental paper prepared with pale brown wash. 194 × 124 mm.
PROVENANCE: J. Richardson, senior (L. 2184); A. Pond; R. Willett; T. Dimsdale; T. Lawrence (L. 2445); W. Esdaile (L. 2617); S. Woodburn; J.C. Robinson; Malcolm (1895–9–15–1275).
LITERATURE: JCR 803; Exh. London, 1894, no. 380; Hind, I, 1915, p. 32, no. 74; Benesch 1187; Exh. London, 1992, no. 62 (with further literature).

One of a series of drawings by Rembrandt that he based on Mughal school miniatures of the seventeenth century. The sources for this and other drawings from Rembrandt's series have been identified in the miniatures that were incorporated in the eighteenth century into the rococo decoration of the *Millionenzimmer* at Schloss Schönbrunn in Vienna. The miniature that formed the basis for the present drawing is dated 1037, which corresponds to 1627–8 of the Christian calendar.

Rembrandt's purpose in making these drawings is unclear but to judge from the twenty-three sheets that survive, his chief interest lay in the costumes. In 1656 he made an etching of *Abraham and the angels* (Bartsch 29) which was inspired by the design copied here.

87 Rembrandt 1606–69

*Landscape with a farm seen through trees on the bank of
a river*

Reed pen and black ink with grey wash on paper washed brown. 162 × 234 mm.
PROVENANCE: Harman (according to JCR – see Lit. below); Andrew James; Malcolm (1895–9–
15–1259).
LITERATURE: JCR 787; Exh. London, 1894, no. 384b; Hind, I, 1915, p. 40, no. 103; Benesch 1244;
Exh. London, 1992, no. 79 (with further literature).

Rembrandt frequently drew the landscape around Amsterdam between the
later 1640s and the mid-1650s. The particular site he sketched here has not
been identified but the drawing belongs to a group of five landscapes he made
in around 1650–53, using a fine nib in a delicate, sparing style on paper
prepared with brown wash. The details in the present work include a haystack
and a lavatory on the left, with a high barn attached to the main building at
the nearer end of the farmhouse.

Drawings of this type may have been intended as finished works of art in
their own right, for independent sale, although Rembrandt himself owned
some books or albums of his landscape studies, which feature in the
inventory of his possessions drawn up by the Amsterdam chamber of
insolvency in 1656.

88 Jan Lievens 1607–74

Forest scene with a large tree by a pool

Pen and brown ink with touches of brown wash and greyish-brown wash. 260 × 411 mm.
PROVENANCE: J.G. Verstolk van Soelen (according to Leembruggen catalogue); G. Leembruggen;
Malcolm (1895–9–15–1198).
LITERATURE: JCR 730; Exh. London, 1894, no. 399; Hind, I, 1915, p. 21, no. 27; Sumowski, VII,
1983, no. 1680$^{\times}$ (with further literature).

A characteristic landscape drawing by Lievens of the type that is sometimes
attributed to his son, Jan Andrea Lievens (b. 1644). The tree on the left
appears in another landscape drawing now in Berlin (KdZ. 13189; Sumowski
no. 1739$^{\times}$, repr.) and another version of the present composition is in the
Ames collection, Saunderstown (Sumowski no. 1679$^{\times}$, repr.). If by the elder
Lievens, these drawings are probably late works.

Jan Lievens studied in Amsterdam with Pieter Lastman, who was also
Rembrandt's master for a short time. From around 1625–31 the two younger
artists worked closely together in their native town, Leiden, possibly sharing
a studio. From 1632–5 Lievens worked in England, where he seems to have
transformed his style under the influence of van Dyck. He was then based in
Antwerp (from 1635–43) before finally settling in Amsterdam.

89 Adriaen van Ostade 1610–85

Village scene: a cottage with a vine, and figures in the street

Pen and brown ink with watercolour and bodycolour. 260 × 220 mm. Signed and dated, lower left: *Av:Ostade.1673*.
PROVENANCE: W. Esdaile (L. 2617); T. Garle; J.C. Robinson (L. 1433); Malcolm (1895–9–15–1239).
LITERATURE: JCR 770; Exh. London, 1894, no. 436; Hind, IV, 1931, p. 17, no. 62; B. Schnackenburg, *Adriaen van Ostade, Isack van Ostade: Zeichnungen und Aquarelle*, 1981, no. 238; Exh. BM, *Adriaen and Isack von Ostade and their Followers*, 1995.

In the 1670s Adriaen van Ostade produced a considerable number of highly finished watercolours of this kind. Writing in 1718, the artist's early biographer, Arnold Houbraken, stated that van Ostade took up the medium after fleeing his Haarlem studio before the advance of the French army in 1672, when he stayed in Amsterdam in the home of a friend, the collector Constantijn Sennepart. A second version of the present composition, also dated 1673, is now in Amsterdam (Historisch Museum). A similar street and cottage appear in a painting of the same year now in Washington (National Gallery of Art).

The children seen in the foreground are inflating a pig's bladder, while the figures behind are traditionally said to be involved in the animal's slaughter, although the details are unclear. Together with the dilapidated state of the building and the overgrown ivy, these motifs may have been read as *vanitas* symbols in the seventeenth century.

Adriaen van Ostade and his younger brother, the short-lived Isack (1621–49), both from Haarlem, reinvigorated the tradition of depicting low-life scenes in the manner of Bruegel. Adriaen was probably taught by Frans Hals (1580/5–1666), with whom Houbraken states that he studied at the same time as another master of peasant scenes, Adriaen Brouwer (1605/6–38).

A: Ostade. 1673.

171

90 Jan Both *c.1615–52*

Landscape with a waterfall

Pen and brown ink with grey wash. 394 × 309 mm. Signed lower right: *J. Both. f.*
PROVENANCE: C.J. Nieuwenhuys; Malcolm (1895–9–15–1126).
LITERATURE: JCR 665; Exh. London, 1894, no. 468; Hind, III, 1926, p. 50, no. 13; J.D. Burke, *Jan Both. Paintings, drawings and prints*, 1976, no. D–25; A.C. Steland, 'Beobachtungen zu frühen Zeichnungen des Jan Both ...', *Niederdeutsche Beiträge zur Kunstgeschichte*, XXVII, 1988, p. 127, fig. 18.

The drawing was employed by Jan Both in two of his paintings, one that was on the Berlin art market in 1928, the other, which agrees only in the right half, in the Rijksmuseum in Amsterdam (inv. no. 591). Yet the drawing seems also to be a finished work in its own right, complete with the artist's signature; it is more elaborate and somewhat larger than most of Both's surviving drawings. The composition, however, is typical, with its idyllic Italianate atmosphere. Stylistically it seems to be a late work.

Jan Both was born in Utrecht, where he studied under Abraham Bloemaert. Like his brother, Andries Both, he travelled to Italy, where Jan is first recorded in 1638. He probably returned to Utrecht in 1641 and spent the remainder of his life there. He specialised in idealised landscapes which were based on Italian scenery, somewhat in the manner of Claude Lorrain.

173

91 Nicolaes Pietersz. Berchem 1620–83

Italian landscape with herdsmen watering cattle

Black chalk with brown wash. 185 × 255 mm. Signed and dated, lower right: *C. Berghem f.1654*
PROVENANCE: J.G. Verstolk van Soelen; King of Holland; G. Leembruggen; Malcolm (1895–9–15–1110).
LITERATURE: JCR 650; Exh. London, 1894, no. 471; Hind, III, 1926, p. 28, no. 9.

A characteristic example of Berchem's finished, independent drawings, of
which he made a considerable number. A print after it was etched, in reverse,
by Jan Visscher (Hollstein 102) and it may always have been Berchem's
intention to have the drawing reproduced in this way. The artist's works were
avidly collected in the eighteenth and nineteenth centuries, and Malcolm
owned no less than fourteen drawings by him.

Berchem was from Haarlem, and is said to have been taught by several
artists, including Jan van Goyen, Nicolaes Moeyaert, Pieter de Grebber and
by Johannes Wils, who was later his father-in-law. In 1642 he entered the
Haarlem painters' guild. His compositions suggest that he travelled to Italy,
although no sojourn there is documented.

174

92 Aelbert Cuyp 1620–91

A village with two windmills by the dunes

Black chalk with pen and black ink, with grey, yellow and yellow-brown wash. 177 × 247 mm.
PROVENANCE: Malcolm (1895–9–15–1139).
LITERATURE: JCR 677; Exh. London, 1894, no. 458; Hind, III, 1926, p. 69, no. 7.

Cuyp frequently made sketches of Dutch towns and the local landscape in the style and medium exhibited here. The somewhat 'panoramic' sense of the composition is also characteristic. Although the drawing must be a topographical view, the town depicted has not been identified; neither is any related painting known.

Cuyp's chalk drawings retain echoes of the style of his second master, Jan van Goyen. Born in Dordrecht, Cuyp was at first a pupil of his own father, a portrait painter. From the early 1640s his oil paintings became more Italianate in composition, although a lack of dated works makes it impossible to reconstruct his stylistic development accurately. Although only recorded in Dordrecht, his paintings and drawings reveal that he travelled widely in the Dutch Republic. After his marriage to a wealthy widow in 1658 he apparently devoted less time to his art and more to fulfilling official functions in his native city.

93 Allart van Everdingen 1621-75

Country scene with thatching and ploughing

Drawn with the brush in grey, with grey wash. 150 × 195 mm. Signed lower right: *AVE*
PROVENANCE: J.C. Robinson; Malcolm (1895-9-15-1157).
LITERATURE: JCR 695; Hind, III, 1926, p. 94, no. 51.

One of a group of four drawings by Everdingen in the Malcolm collection
that are thought to represent the *Four Seasons* (Hind 48-51). The present
drawing would have been intended for winter. The tradition for representing
the seasons in this way was a strong one in Netherlandish art and can be
traced to late medieval manuscript illuminations. Like the majority of van
Everdingen's drawings, the present sheet would probably have been an
independent work rather than a preparatory study for a painting or print.

Everdingen was a prolific landscape draughtsman as well as a painter and
etcher. He came originally from Alkmaar but studied at first with Roelandt
Savery (1576-1639), probably in Utrecht. He spent the first part of his
independent career in Haarlem, where he was also a pupil of Pieter Molijn
(1595-1661). In 1644 he visited Scandinavia, where the scenery had a
profound effect on his art, and from 1652 he lived in Amsterdam.

94 Lambert Doomer 1624–1700

The Dumbkes Gate at Anrath

Pen and brown ink with touches of brown, yellow-brown and grey wash. 149 × 187 mm.
Inscribed by the artist in pen and brown ink, top centre: *dÿmbkes poort tot Anraet*
PROVENANCE: C. Ploos van Amstel; Muller (according to Leembruggen catalogue);
G. Leembruggen; Malcolm (1895–9–15–1147).
LITERATURE: JCR 685; Hind, I, 1915, no. 4; Sumowski, II, 1979, no. 402 (with further
literature).

Lambert Doomer drew numerous views of Anrath, where he had relatives.
His father, a frame-maker whose portrait was painted by Rembrandt, was
born in the town (the portrait is now in the Metropolitan Museum of Art,
New York). Doomer's drawings are difficult to date and he may have visited
Anrath on several occasions, but the present watercolour is thought to be
from the early 1660s. The artist possessed a volume of his drawings, recorded
in the inventory of his estate, entitled the *Doomer-Hoff*, in which his views
of Anrath may have been kept.

Doomer was possibly a pupil of Rembrandt in the first half of the 1640s,
although no documentary evidence supports the connection. Yet the style of
his numerous landscape drawings seems to depend on the master from
Amsterdam, the town where Doomer himself was mostly active. He also
travelled to France in 1645–6 and to Germany in around 1663 on drawing
expeditions.

95 Jacob van Ruisdael 1628/9–82

View in Alkmaar, with the Grote Kerk

Black chalk with grey wash. 200 × 310 mm. Inscribed, lower right: *Ruisdael* and on the *verso: Te Alkmaar agter de Groote Kerk*
PROVENANCE: J.G. Verstolk van Soelen; G. Leembruggen; Malcolm (1895-9-15-1296).
LITERATURE: JCR 822; Exh. London, 1894, no. 456; Hind, IV, 1931, p. 40, no. 5; Exh. London, 1972, no. 259; Exh. Amsterdam, Rijksmuseum and Toronto, Art Gallery of Ontario, *The Dutch Cityscape*, 1977, no. 78; J. Giltaij, 'De tekeningen van Jacob van Ruisdael', *Oud Holland*, XCIV, 1980, pp. 154 and 197–8, no. 76; E.J. Walford, *Jacob van Ruisdael and the Perception of Landscape*, 1991, pp. 7 and 93, fig. 87.

The drawing shows the Gasthuisstraat behind the church of St Lawrence (the *Grote Kerk* or *St Laurenskerk*) at Alkmaar in north-western Holland. It is a characteristic example of Ruisdael's draughtsmanship when producing a finished composition and is not related to any of his paintings or etchings. Ruisdael may have toured parts of Holland in the early 1650s, making, among others, this drawing and studies of Egmond Castle. One of the latter, now in Stuttgart (inv. no. C64/1329), was used by him in his celebrated painting of the *Jewish Cemetery* now in Dresden, which was probably painted in the mid-1650s (the version now in Detroit, which does not depend on the drawing in Stuttgart, is probably later).

Jacob van Ruisdael was born and at first worked in Haarlem, where he probably studied under his father Isaack and his uncle Salomon. From 1657 he lived in Amsterdam, although as his works reveal he travelled elsewhere in Holland and Germany. In 1721 his biographer Arnold Houbraken wrote that he used to perform surgical operations in Amsterdam and he may have practised this second profession; in 1676 'Jacobus Rijsdael' secured a degree in medicine in Caen, and was inscribed in the list of doctors in Amsterdam.

96 Ludolf Bakhuizen 1631–1708

A yacht before the coast at Plymouth

Pen and black ink with grey wash. 252 × 343 mm. Signed upper left: *Ludolph Bakhuizen f'*.
Dated lower left: *1679*.
PROVENANCE: J.G. Verstolk van Soelen; G. Leembruggen; Malcolm (1895–9–15–1097).
LITERATURE: JCR 637; Exh. London, 1894, no. 450; Hind, III, 1926, p. 15, no. 16; Exh.
Amsterdam, Nederlands Scheepvaart Museum, *Ludolf Bakhuizen*, 1985, no. T9.

The drawing is one of many highly finished works executed largely with the
brush that Bakhuizen completed in the 1670s and 1680s. The Union flags and
St George's cross identify the foreground vessel as English, and it could be
the royal yacht that in 1677 brought Charles II from Portsmouth to
Plymouth. The coast near the latter is represented: the cliff in the centre
capped by a building shows Mount Edgcumbe, with Cawsend Bay to the left.
A related painting, dated one year later in 1680, is in the Bayerische
Staatsgemäldesammlung, Munich (inv. no. 2007).

Ludolf Bakhuizen was a specialist painter of maritime subjects. Unlike his
contemporaries Willem van de Velde the Elder and the Younger, he is not
known to have worked in England and the present drawing must depend on
another depiction of the Devon coast. He was based for most of his life in
Amsterdam, and became the leading Dutch marine painter after the van de
Veldes settled in England in 1672.

97 Frans van Mieris the Elder 1635–81

Willem Paedts as an infant, with his nurse

Black chalk on vellum. 296 × 233 mm. Inscribed below: *F. van Mieris, Anno 1664*
PROVENANCE: W. Paedts; S. Feitema the Younger; G. Hoet the Younger; van Tol; Muilman; Neyman; Nogaret; Joullain; H. van Eyl-Sluyter; J.C. Robinson; Malcolm (1895–9–15–1210).
LITERATURE: Literature: JCR 742; Exh. London, 1894, no, 423; Hind, III, 1926, p. 144, no. 3; J.G. van Gelder in W. Strauss (ed.), *Tribute to Wolfgang Stechow*, 1976, pp. 70–73 (with further literature).

This exceptional work by Frans van Mieris the Elder, few of whose drawings survive, was identified in the sale of Gerard Hoet in 1760 as follows: 'A baby in the cradle, with his wet nurse and other details. Of an astonishing perfection and delicacy, drawn from the life in black chalk, being Mr Paats in the cradle, A° 1664.' The catalogue further states that it was a well-known work by van Mieris and that Hoet had bought it twice, firstly at the posthumous sale of Willem Paedts in Leiden, and later from the Feitema collection. In the latter's sale catalogue of 1758, the infant depicted is not named, but the identification is confirmed by a second study by van Mieris (now in the Fondation Custodia in Paris, F. Lugt collection) of what appears to be the same child in the same cradle. This second drawing was described in the sale of J. van der Marck in 1773 as a study of Paedts. It is also correctly dated 1665, the year of Willem Paedts' birth; the inscription on the present sheet, which was perhaps added later, is inaccurate in this respect.

Willem Paedts (1665–1750) was a prominent citizen of Leiden, holding several important local offices including that of burgomaster, a post he occupied seven times. The son of Cornelis Paedts and his wife Agatha, née Couwenhoven, the name of his wet-nurse, shown here, has not been recorded. Cornelis Paedts is known to have received drawing lessons from van Mieris, who was therefore the obvious recipient of the present commission. The artist studied with Gerrit Dou, Rembrandt's pupil, who founded the Leiden tradition of detailed paintings with an enamel-smooth finish (*fijnschilderij*), of which van Mieris became a leading exponent.

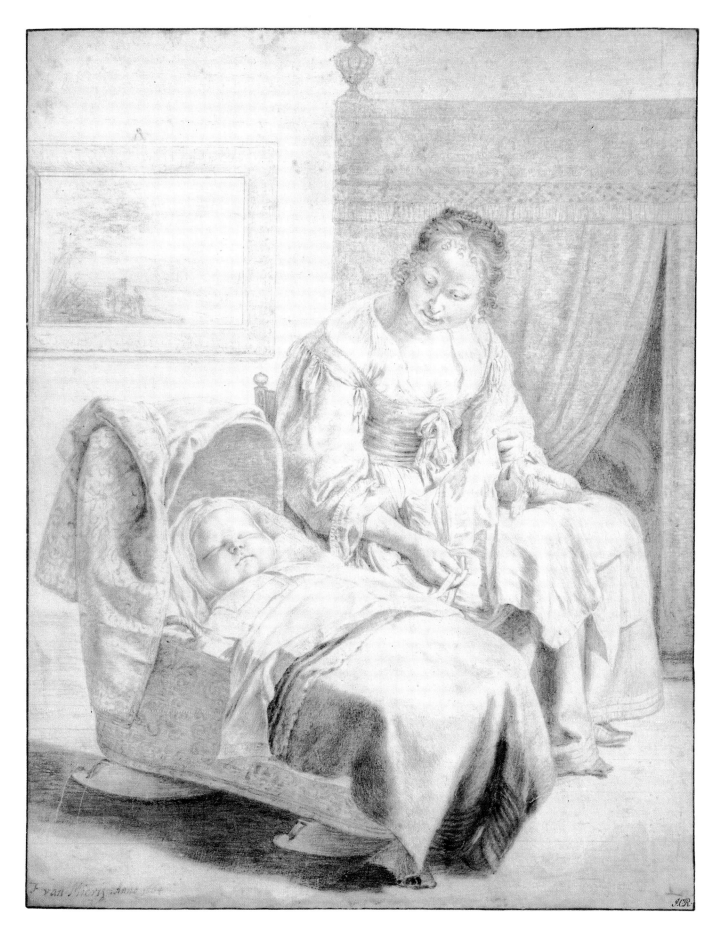

98 Adriaen van de Velde 1636–72

A cavalier on horseback

Red chalk. 290 × 195 mm. Signed or inscribed lower left: *A Van de Velde* [?]
PROVENANCE: P.H. Lankrink (L. 2090 and *Suppl.*); Malcolm (1895–9–15–1330).
LITERATURE: JCR 855; Exh. London, 1894, no. 463; Hind, IV, 1931, p. 74, no. 1; Exh. London, 1984, no. 103.

Adriaen van de Velde used his numerous figure-studies from models posed in his studio as a stock of motifs that he could employ in his paintings (see William W. Robinson, 'Preparatory Drawings by Adriaen van de Velde', *Master Drawings*, XVII, 1979, pp. 3–23). The drawings, almost all in red chalk, are difficult to order chronologically and those that he used may date from long before the paintings to which they are related. To add further motifs to his stock, he frequently made offsets of his drawings, a fate that may have befallen the present sheet, to judge from the evenness of the chalk surface. Characteristically, he here captures an Italianate quality of light, somewhat in the manner of Nicolaes Berchem (on whom see no. 91).

Adriaen van de Velde was the son and brother of the celebrated marine painters Willem van de Velde the Elder and the Younger. He spent most of his life in Amsterdam, but according to Arnold Houbraken he studied with Jan Wijnants in Haarlem. He may also have been his father's pupil, and his subject-matter suggests that he visited Italy, although no other record of the journey survives. Most of his paintings, etchings and drawings are of landscapes, with prominent figures and animals, but he also produced religious, allegorical, mythological and *genre* subjects, as well as portraits.

99 Jan van der Heyden 1637–1712

A large building on fire

Pen and brown ink with grey wash. 322 × 422 mm.
PROVENANCE: J.C. Robinson (L. 1433); Malcolm (1895–9–15–1171).
LITERATURE: JCR 706; Exh. London, 1894, no. 447; Hind, III, 1926, p. 115, no. 4; H. Wagner, *Jan van der Heyden*, 1971, p. 39.

The drawing is a preparatory study for an engraving by J. Mulder. The print was probably published in 1690, at the same time as the book van der Heyden produced with his son Jan the Younger, describing the fire-prevention techniques he had invented, including the fire-hose (*Beschryving der nieuwlijks uitgevonden en ge-octrojeerde Slang-Brand-Spuiten*).

The view is a *capriccio*, combining invented buildings with others that are based on identifiable structures. The church on the left is fictitious and appears again in a painting by van der Heyden now in a private collection, which contains further buildings based on edifices in Cologne (Wagner, *op. cit.*, no. 63). Yet the small shelter attached to the church represents a structure that was annexed to the *Oude Kerk* (Old Church) in Amsterdam. Behind it, the arcaded gallery is reminiscent of the old Amsterdam Stock Exchange, while the burning building is another invention; it also appears on a drawing in the Rijksmuseum and on a related print of 1677 that was published to advertise van der Heyden's and his brother Nicolaes' then newly invented fire-hose. At the far end of the square, the building with a tall pitched roof is based on the Amsterdam fish-market. The gate on the right resembles that depicted by van der Heyden in views of Veere (Wagner nos 72 and 76), while the small pyramid, based on that of Sestius in Rome, also appears in a painted *capriccio* now in the John G. Johnson Collection in Philadelphia (Wagner no. 158).

Van der Heyden is chiefly remembered for his meticulously painted topographical paintings. Most of them represent Amsterdam, where he was mainly active, but others depict towns elsewhere in the Netherlands and in the Rhineland. From 1668 he seems to have concentrated on mechanical and engineering work, being at various times in charge of street-lighting and firefighting in Amsterdam.

100 Jacob Cats 1741–99

Landscape with peasants and cattle by a farm

Watercolour. 360 × 470 mm. Signed and dated, *verso: J. Cats inv et fec^t 1796*
PROVENANCE: J.H. Hawkins; W.B. Tiffin; Malcolm (1895–9–15–1135).
LITERATURE: JCR 673; Hind, IV, 1931, p. 157, no. 10.

Jacob Cats made a large number of highly-detailed watercolours at the end of
the eighteenth century, taking a variety of motifs, both urban and rural, as
his subject-matter. Although John Malcolm collected few eighteenth-century
drawings, he had two by Cats, to whose work he may have been attracted by
Cats' stylistic links with seventeenth-century landscape painters such as Jan
van der Heyden and Adriaen van de Velde.

  Cats' family settled in Amsterdam when he was a boy, and he began as a
painter of decorative interior wall-hangings. His second master, Gerard van
Rossum (1699/1700–1772), owned a large collection of prints and drawings
which his pupil studied with profit. As an independent painter, Cats often
worked with Egbert van Drielst (1745–1818) and he increasingly turned to
making drawings as the demand for paintings decreased among Dutch
collectors of the period.

Appendix

List of further drawings exhibited (in brackets the last part of the register number is given; all are prefixed with the numbers 1895–9–15–). The drawings are listed alphabetically by school.

ITALIAN DRAWINGS   catalogues reg.no.
     1895-9-15-

Andrea del Sarto, *Pietà with four Saints*   JCR 109 (546)

Cavaliere d'Arpino, *Self-Portrait*   JCR 223, G & P 26 (664)

Bandinelli, B., *Noah*   JCR 112 (549)

Fra Bartolommeo, *Drapery study*   JCR 22 (458)

Fra Bartolommeo, *The Risen Christ with four figures*
   JCR 91 (528)

Bonsignori, F., *Kneeling woman*   JCR 104 (541)

Botticelli, S., *Faith*   JCR 12, P & P 25 (448)

Campagnola, D., *Figures in a Landscape*   JCR 388 (836)

Campi, B., *Music-making angel*   (746)

Cantarini, S., *Bishop kneeling before a vision of the Virgin and Child*   JCR 277 (717)

Carracci, An., *Portrait of Camillo Borghese*   JCR 252 (693)

Clovio, G., *Lamentation*   JCR 213, G & P 70 (654)

Credi, L. di,. *Head of a Boy*   JCR 26, P & P 50 (462)

Faccini, P., *Virgin and Child with Saints*   JCR 257 (698)

Ferrari, Gaudenzio, *Head of the Virgin*   JCR 319 (766)

Ferri, C., *Crucifixion*   JCR 224 (665)

Florentine School XV cent., circle of, *Youth drawing*
   JCR 4, P & P 278 (440)

del Garbo, R., *The Circumcision*   JCR 33, P & P 65 (469)

Garofalo, *Virgin and Child with Saints*   JCR 343 (790)

Giovanni Agostino da Lodi, *Head of a man*   JCR 43 (481)

Guercino, *Charity*   JCR 266 (706)

Guercino, *Cupid*   JCR 267 (707)

Girolamo di Benvenuto, *The Delphic Sibyl*
   JCR App. I, 20, P & P 78 (1394)

Girolamo di Benvenuto, *The Cimmerian Sibyl,*
   JCR App. I, 21, P & P 79 (1395)

Leonardo da Vinci, *Two studies of a cat and a dog*
   JCR 41, P & P 101 (477)

Leonardo da Vinci, *Allegory with Fortune*
   JCR 44, P & P 104 (482)

Lippi, F., *Two men*   JCR 18, P & P 136 (454)

Lomazzo, A., attrib. to, *Allegorical female figure*
   JCR 322 (769)

Mantegna, A., school of, *Hercules and Antaeus*
   JCR 335, P & P 162 (782)

Michelangelo, *The Flagellation of Christ*   JCR 63, W.15 (500)

Michelangelo, *Crucifixion*   JCR 72, W.81 (509)

Michelangelo, *Last Judgement*   JCR 80, W.60 (518)

Michelangelo, *Portrait of Andrea Quaratesi*
   JCR 82, W.59 (519)

Moro, M. Agnolo del, *Esther and Ahasuerus*   JCR 349 (796)

Orsi, L., *Allegory of sleep*   JCR 302, P.46 (743)

Palma Vecchio, J., *The Holy Family*   JCR 363 (810)

Piazza, C., *Madonna and Child with Saints*   JCR 348 (795)

Primaticcio, F., *Minerva (or Bellona) carried to Olympus*
   JCR 236 (677)

Raffaellino da Reggio, *Self-Portrait (?)*
   JCR 218, G & P 238 (659)

Raphael, *Lamentation*   P & G 10 (636)

Raphael, *Venus*   JCR 190, P & G 27 (629)

Roncalli, C., *Putti*   JCR 292, P & G 253 (732)

Sienese School, second half of the fourteenth century, *Christ and the woman of Samaria*   JCR 239, P & P 269 (680)

Signorelli, L., *Three shepherds and an angel*
   JCR 165, P & P 235 (602)

Schiavone, A., *Judith*   JCR 405 (854)

Sodoma, *St Catherine*   JCR 317 (764)

Titian, *St Eustace*   JCR 371 (818)

Veronese, P., *Altarpiece with dead Christ*   JCR 393 (841)

Viti, T., *Study for the Arrivabene altarpiece*
   JCR 169, P & G 258 (606)

Zuccaro, F., *The raising of the son of the widow of Nain*
   JCR 136, G & P 297 (573)

Zucchi, J., attrib. to, *Three Graces*   JCR 560 (1018)

SPANISH DRAWINGS

Berruguete, A., *Virgin standing on clouds*   JCR 417 (866)

Murillo, B.E., *Adoration of the Infant Christ*   (891)

de Pereda, A., *St. Jerome*   JCR 432 (883)

FRENCH DRAWINGS

Boucher, F., *Pastoral scene*   JCR 501 (954)

Claude Lorrain, *S. Agnese fuori le mure*   JCR 452, H.99 (905)

Claude Lorrain, *Jacob and Rachel at the well*
   JCR 454, H.270 (907)

Claude Lorrain, *Landscape with Rest on the Flight*
   JCR 449, H.267 (902)

Claude Lorrain, *Landscape with Rest on the Flight*
   JCR 448, H.254 (901)

Claude Lorrain, *Coast view*   JCR 458, H.198 (911)

Clouet, F., *Portrait of the Duc de Rohan*   JCR 441 (894)

La Fage, N.-R., *A Roman battle*   JCR 498 (951)

Watteau, A., *Heads of two daughters of Sirois*
   JCR 490, P.22 (942)

Watteau. A., *Five studies of seated woman*
   JCR 492, P.3 (944)

GERMAN DRAWINGS

Aachen, Hans von, *The Entombment of Christ*
   JCR 563 (1026)

Dürer, A., *Death riding a horse*   JCR 518, Rowlands 163 (971)

Dürer, A., circle of, *Lily of the valley*
   JCR 530, Rowlands 262 (986)

Franck, H., *Soldiers storming a fortress*
   JCR 515, Rowlands 286 (968)

Holbein, H. the Elder, *Sigmund Holbein*
   JCR 5, Rowlands 302 (987)

Master of the Drapery Studies, *Figure and drapery*
JCR 512, Rowlands 8 (965)

Plepp, H.J., *Heraldic design for glass*   JCR 540 (996)

Schongauer, M., *Man with a book*
JCR 508, Rowlands 17 (961)

NETHERLANDISH DRAWINGS

Anon. Flemish XV cent., *The Adoration of the Magi*
JCR 548, P.3 (1006)

Anon. Flemish XV cent., *Two kneeling ladies*
JCR 550, P.10 (1008)

Berchem, N., *Falconer's halt*   JCR 652, H.34 (1112)

Berchem, N., *Italian peasants at an inn*
JCR 653, H.35 (1113)

Bisschop, Jan de, *Portrait of Admiral Vlugh*
JCR 660, H.9 (1121)

Bray, J. de, *Portrait of Maria van Teffelen*
JCR 668, H.5 (1129)

Bril, P., *A tree*   P.3 (1373)

Brueghel, J., *A vase with flowers*   JCR 554, H.10 (1012)

Dusart, C., *Tavern scene*   JCR 834, H.2 (1309)

Eeckhout, G. van den, *A youth seated, looking upwards*
JCR 759, H.147 (1228)

Esselens, J., *Music party in a garden*   JCR 690, H.2 (1152)

Everdingen, A. van, *Scene on a Dutch Coast (Autumn?)*
JCR 694, H.50 (1156)

Flinck, G., *A man playing the lute*   JCR 699, H.3 (1161)

Goltzius, H. *The Temptation*   JCR 561, P.7 (1019)

Goyen, J. van, *River bank with boats*   JCR 700, H.3 (1162)

Helmbreker, D., *Supposed self-portrait*   JCR 712, H.1 (1177)

Laar, P. van, *Halt of gypsies*   JCR 726, H.2 (1194)

Maas, D., *Woodland road*   JCR 737, H.19 (1205)

Maes, N., *The Holy Family, after Rembrandt*
JCR 732, H.5 (1200)

Molyn, P., *Landscape with haymaking* JCR 749, H.10 (1217)

Molyn, P., *A village road*   JCR 751, H.11 (1219)

Moucheron, I. de, *A garden terrace*   JCR 755, H.11 (1224)

Netscher, C., *Young man seated at a table*
JCR 758, H.3 (1227)

Ostade, I. van, *Interior of a barber's shop*
JCR 891, H.2 (1371)

Rembrandt, *A man in a high cap*   JCR 791, H.18 (1263)

Rembrandt, *A serving woman with candle*
JCR 796, H.51 (1268)

Roghman, R., *The castle of Montfoort* JCR 815, H.23 (1289)

Romeyn, W., *Herdsmen at Tivoli*   JCR 818, H.3 (1292)

Slingelandt, P. van, *Study of a young woman*
JCR 836, H.1 (1311)

Swanevelt, H. van, *Italian landscape*   JCR 840, H.15 (1315)

Velde, A. van de, *Woman seated, with cattle*
JCR 848, H.12 (1323)

Velde, A. van de, *Peasants and cattle by a fountain*
JCR 849, H.13 (1324)

Velde, E. van de, *The quay of a Dutch canal*
JCR 846, H.2 (1321)

Velde, E. van de, *Party in grounds of a château*
JCR 847, H.3 (1322)

Visscher, C., *Portrait of a middle-aged man*
JCR 871, H.3 (1346)

Waterloo, A., *View of Utrecht*   JCR 876, H.21 (1354)

Zeeman, R., *Sea-piece with three-master*
JCR 890, H.10 (1370)

Bibliography
Literature Cited in Abbreviated Form

Exhibition catalogues are listed under 'Exh.' and arranged alphabetically by town and by date.

Bartsch = A. Bartsch, *Catalogue raisonné de toutes les estampes qui forment l'oeuvre de Rembrandt [. . .]*, Vienna, 1797 and *Le peintre-graveur*, 21 vols, Vienna, 1803–21.

Benesch = O. Benesch, *The Drawings of Rembrandt*, 2nd edn revised by E. Benesch, 6 vols, London, 1973.

Degenhart and Schmitt = B. Degenhart and A. Schmitt, *Corpus der Italienischen Zeichnungen 1300–1450. Teil I: Süd- und Mittelitalien*, Berlin, 1968.

Exh. Adelaide and Melbourne, 1980 = N. Turner and M. Royalton-Kisch, *Leonardo, Michelangelo and the Century of Genius*, Art Gallery of South Australia and National Gallery of Victoria.

Exh. Leningrad and Moscow, 1977 = N. Turner and M. Kisch, *Italian XVIth Century Drawings from the British Museum*, Hermitage and Pushkin Museum.

Exh. London, 1894 = S. Colvin, *Guide to an Exhibition of Drawings and Sketches by the Old Masters, principally from the Malcolm Collection [. . .]*, British Museum.

Exh. London, 1972 = E. Croft-Murray, *The Art of Drawing*, British Museum.

Exh. London, 1974 = J.A. Gere (ed.), *Portrait Drawings XV–XX Centuries*, British Museum.

Exh. London, 1975 = J.A. Gere and N. Turner, *Drawings by Michelangelo*, British Museum.

Exh. London, 1980 = P. Hulton, *Watteau Drawings in the British Museum*, British Museum.

Exh. London, 1983 = J.A. Gere and N. Turner, *Drawings by Raphael from [. . .] English collections*, British Museum.

Exh. London, 1984 = J. Rowlands (ed.), *Master Drawings and Watercolours in the British Museum*, British Museum.

Exh. London, 1986 = N. Turner, *Florentine drawings of the sixteenth century*, British Museum.

Exh. London, 1988 = J. Rowlands, with the assistance of Giulia Bartrum, *The Age of Dürer and Holbein: German Drawings 1400–1550*, British Museum.

Exh. London, 1992 = M. Royalton-Kisch, *Drawings by Rembrandt and his Circle in the British Museum*, British Museum.

Exh. London, 1994 = N. Turner, *The Study of Italian Drawings, the contribution of Philip Pouncey*, British Museum.

Exh. Paris, 1978–9 = J.A. Gere and R. Bacou, *Claude Lorrain. Dessins du British Museum*, Musée du Louvre.

Exh. Tokyo and Nagoya, 1996 = M. Koshikawa and H. Kurita, *Italian 16th and 17th century Drawings from the British Museum*, Tokyo, The National Museum of Western Art, Nagoya, Aichi Prefectural Museum of Art.

Gere and Pouncey = J.A. Gere and P.M.R. Pouncey with the assistance of Rosalind Wood, *Italian Drawings in the Department of Prints and Drawings in the British Museum. Artists working in Rome c.1550 to c.1640*, London, 1983.

Giampaolo and Muzzi = M. di Giampaolo and A. Muzzi, *Correggio, i disegni*, Turin, 1988.

Gould = C. Gould, *The Paintings of Correggio*, London, 1976.

Hind = A.M. Hind, *Catalogue of Dutch and Flemish Drawings in the Department of Prints and Drawings in the British Museum*, vols I-IV, London, 1915–31.

Hind, 1926 = A.M. Hind, *Catalogue of the Drawings of Claude Lorrain [. . .] in the British Museum*, London, 1926.

Hollstein = F.W.H. Hollstein, *Dutch and Flemish Etchings, Engravings and Woodcuts, c.1450–1700*, Amsterdam, 1947 etc (in progress).

JCR = J.C. Robinson, *Descriptive Catalogue of Drawings by the Old Masters forming the Collection of John Malcolm of Poltalloch*, London, 2nd edn, 1876.

Joannides = P. Joannides, *The Drawings of Raphael with a Complete Catalogue*, Oxford, 1983.

L. = F. Lugt, *Les marques de collections de dessins et d'estampes*, Amsterdam, 1921, with *Supplément*, The Hague, 1956.

Parker, 1930 = K.T. Parker, 'The Drawings of Antoine Watteau in the British Museum', *Old Master Drawings*, V, 1930, pp. 1–28.

Parker and Mathey = K.T. Parker and J. Mathey, *Antoine Watteau. Catalogue complet de son oeuvre dessiné*, 2 vols, Paris, 1957.

Popham 1932 = A.E. Popham, *Catalogue of Drawings by Dutch and Flemish Artists [. . .] in the British Museum*, vol. V, London, 1932.

Popham 1967 = A.E. Popham, *Italian Drawings in the [. . .] British Museum. Artists working in Parma in the Sixteenth Century*, London, 1967.

Popham and Pouncey = A.E. Popham and P.M.R. Pouncey, *Italian Drawings in the [. . .] British Museum. The Fourteenth and Fifteenth Centuries*, London, 1950.

Pouncey and Gere = P.M.R. Pouncey and J.A. Gere, *Italian Drawings in the [. . .] British Museum. Raphael and his Circle*, 2 vols, London, 1962.

Robertson = G. Robertson, *Giovanni Bellini*, New York, 1981.

Robinson, see JCR.

Roethlisberger = M. Roethlisberger, *Claude Lorrain. The Drawings*, 2 vols, Berkeley and Los Angeles, 1968.

Rowlands = J. Rowlands, with the assistance of Giulia Bartrum, *Drawings by German Artists [. . .] in the British Museum: the fifteenth century and the sixteenth century*, 2 vols, London, 1993.

Sumowski = W. Sumowski, *Drawings of the Rembrandt School*, vols I-X, New York, 1979–92 (in progress).

de Tolnay = C. de Tolnay, *Corpus dei Disegni di Michelangelo*, vols I-III, Novara, 1975–8.

Turner = N. Turner, *Italian Baroque Drawings*, London, 1980.

Wethey = H. Wethey, *Titian and his Drawings [. . .]*, Princeton, 1987.

Wilde = J. Wilde, *Italian Drawings in the [. . .] British Museum. Michelangelo and his Studio*, London, 1953.

Index of Artists